The Easter Rebellion
1916 A NEW ILLUSTRATED HISTORY

In the wake of the Easter Rebellion of 1916, a generation of extraordinary revolutionaries left behind a wealth of photographs, sketches, posters and cartoons, as well as eyewitness accounts, manuscripts, personal notebooks and letters. From photographs of young men proudly parading with guns landed at Howth in 1914, to the leaders' final letters to their loved ones in the hours before their execution, this first-hand material gives an immediacy and an intimacy to these iconic moments. Now, for the first time, it is gathered together and accompanied by a compelling and authoritative exploration of the indelible events of Easter Week.

Dr Conor McNamara is 1916 Scholar in Residence at the National University of Ireland, Galway. He was senior researcher for the University of Notre Dame's 1916 television series to be aired in March 2016. His other books include *Easter 1916: A Research Guide* (2015) and *The West of Ireland in the Nineteenth Century: New Perspectives* (2011).

Lyrics of the political ballad 'Who Fears to Speak of Easter Week?' by Maria Giddons, published in 1916 and decorated with drawings by Peter Rigney. NLI

The Easter Rebellion 1916
A NEW ILLUSTRATED HISTORY

Conor McNamara

The Collins Press

First published in 2015 by
The Collins Press
West Link Park
Doughcloyne
Wilton
Cork

Reprinted 2016

A CIP record for this book is available from the British Library.

ISBN: 978-1-84889-2590

Design (including cover) and typesetting by Burns Design
Typeset in Baskerville
Printed in Poland by Białostockie Zakłady Graficzne SA

COVER IMAGES
FRONT AND SPINE: The effect of sniper fire on one of Dublin's Georgian windows.
BACK: O'Connell Bridge, 1916. NLI

CONTENTS

Sackville Street (now O'Connell Street) lies in ruins, 1916. NLI

1

INTRODUCTION: GLORIOUS FOREVER?

I have met them at close of day
Coming with vivid faces
From counter or desk among grey
Eighteenth-century houses.
I have passed with a nod of the head
Or polite meaningless words,
Or have lingered awhile and said
Polite meaningless words,
And thought before I had done
Of a mocking tale or a gibe
To please a companion
Around the fire at the club,
Being certain that they and I
But lived where motley is worn:
All changed, changed utterly:
A terrible beauty is born.

'Easter, 1916' | W. B. Yeats | 25 September 1916

T HE CONCEPT OF CONFLICT was ingrained in western European intellectual thought at the opening of the twentieth century. Empires endured because they were prepared to sacrifice their soldiers on the field of battle.[1] The validity of a national group's claim for political independence was measured by its willingness and capacity to inflict and endure violence. Irish separatists' preoccupation with national resurrection and sacrifice reflected the contemporary mainstream of European intellectual culture, rather than a uniquely Irish backwater.[2] The 1916 Rising was orchestrated to assert Ireland's claim for independence in the midst of a European war that was reshaping the world and inflicting unprecedented carnage. Clandestinely planned by a self-appointed group that regarded itself as representing the true Irish nation, the Rising was intended as much to shake off historical lethargy and to inspire future generations as to achieve immediate autonomy. In terms of loss of human life, the Easter Rising shrinks in comparison to the appalling slaughter witnessed across Europe in 1916; fewer than 800 people died during Easter Week, while over 19,000 perished on the first day of the Battle of the Somme alone.[3]

The significance of the Easter Rebellion derives from the fact that it was an explicit and highly publicised repudiation of the British Empire by white, anglophone subjects at the heart of the United Kingdom. The Rising refuted the logic of British rule in Ireland in the most public manner possible, deliberately challenging the Allies' claim to be 'fighting for the fate of small nations'. The rebels' willingness to assert Ireland's claim for independence through insurrection, as well as their preoccupation with courage and national redemption, reflected contemporary European fears that the effete modern generation of young men needed to 'rediscover' their masculinity and reassert their capacity to defend national honour. The proliferation of militarism in Europe at this time reflected not only 'the cult of discipline', but a reaction against the widely perceived decadence of the era.[4]

New Nationalism and the Language of Revolt

The early twentieth century witnessed the political emergence in Ireland of a generation of educated lower-middle-class Catholic revolutionaries determined to reverse the humiliations of the old century. While the Irish Parliamentary Party dominated politics for several decades and aspired to capture the levers of state through Home Rule, Patrick Pearse and his 'rising generation' sought to create a reinvigorated Irish nationalism rather than merely seize control of the levers of state. In this respect, rebellion assumed many forms other than political violence: playing Gaelic games, learning the Irish language, singing Irish songs rather than music hall ditties, and favouring Irish produce over imported British goods were all part of a wider process of constructing a rejuvenated cultural identity. Sport disseminated the nationalist cultural revival: only two years after its foundation in 1884, the Gaelic Athletic Association (GAA) already had 50,000 members and 400 affiliated clubs.[5]

The Gaelic League was founded in 1893 to preserve the Irish language. Its newspaper, *An Claidheamh Soluis*, was founded in 1899 with language scholar Eoin Mac Néill as editor. By 1908, the movement had 671 Irish branches, with at least one in every county, and at its height 75,000 members enjoyed Irish language classes, the singing of Irish songs and Irish dancing. Competitions, *feiseanna*, *céilithe* and concerts provided a lively array of occasions for members to socialise, compete and show off. The movement proved adept at attracting young, lower-middle-class Catholics: it was supported by respectable community leaders, including teachers and priests, which crucially allowed young women to attend and socialise without attracting odium.[6]

Despite the significant achievements of the Gaelic League and the GAA in the closing decades of the nineteenth century, activists believed that Irish culture still languished as a mere pallid imitation of British popular culture. The Irish cultural revival represented broad strata of artists: the 1907 riots over J. M. Synge's play *The Playboy of the Western World* were symptomatic of a wider struggle to control representations of the 'authentic Irish nation'. The GAA and the Gaelic League shared overlapping memberships and both organisations moulded the popular perception of what constituted 'authentic' Irish cultural pursuits.[7]

For Pearse and others of his milieu, culture represented a seminal battlefield. The failure of previous generations of revolutionaries was a national stain that could only be erased through revolution, and those who were unwilling to make personal sacrifices could not expect a place in the

CHRISTMAS 1884.—(See Page 4)

John Bull beholds a vision of the near future

new revolutionary dispensation. The Irish Volunteers were conceived as a nationalist militia, but also as a component of a wider cultural awakening. In the evolving language of revolution, popular adherence to conventional nationalism was regarded as a symptom of cultural malaise. Piaras Béaslaí claimed that before the rise of physical-force nationalism:

> All faith in lofty ideals, in patriotism or self-sacrifice seemed to have vanished and horrible cynicism reigned everywhere. The place hunter seemed supreme. The faithful few who strove to keep the torch burning in those dark days – the torch handed down from Tone and Emmet – were met on every side with derision. A weak supine corrupt party seemed to speak for and have the confidence of the vast majority of Irish people.[8]

To Patrick Pearse, Joseph Plunkett, Thomas MacDonagh and others, the Irish Republican Brotherhood (IRB) – a secret society dedicated to the complete separation of Ireland from the British Empire – was inseparable from, and inconceivable without, this wider cultural struggle for the 'salvation' of Ireland. Pearse claimed in 1914: 'It is more than a historically great struggle that is going on in Ireland. It is a battle of two nations. We have to undo the English conquest of Ireland. We have to re-establish in Ireland her supremacy. And so the Irish movement in Ireland is not only a political movement. It is something much larger and more complicated.' For Pearse, the education system denigrated Gaelic culture, and consequently Irish manhood and national self-respect. The system 'was intended to breed a generation of slaves' and 'there came into Ireland a great vulgarity'.[9]

Shortly after the Rebellion, *The 1916 Poets*, featuring the work of Pearse, Plunkett and MacDonagh, became an instant bestseller in Ireland. The book raced through several reissues, the poems were taught in Catholic schools, and most families with nationalist leanings possessed a copy. When assessing the ideas influencing the 1916 Rebellion, later critics turned to the readily accessible poetry of these writers rather than researching the political writings of the Volunteer leaders.[10] Retrospective analysis of the rebel

FACING PAGE: For most Irish nationalists, Home Rule, rather than complete separation from Britain, represented the limits of political ambition. This cartoon of Romantic Ireland was published in Dublin by *The Freeman's Journal* in December 1884. NLI

SUPPLEMENT GIVEN AWAY WITH THE "WEEKLY FREEMAN" OF DECEMBER 16TH 1882

A VISION OF CO ING EVENTS.

ABOVE AND FACING PAGE: Ireland, depicted as Róisín Dubh or Caitlín Ní Houlihan, awaits Home Rule. Published by *The Freeman's Journal* in December 1888. NLI

leaders' literary writings briefly sustained the illusion of 'the soldier as failed artist'. Thomas MacDonagh joined the Volunteers shortly after their formation in 1913 and his political views were initially moderate. So were those of his close friend Joseph Plunkett. MacDonagh was the least senior of the seven signatories of the 1916 Proclamation, but his poetry and drama have been interpreted as an indication of a greater knowledge of the conspiracy on his part. MacDonagh's *When the Dawn Is Come*, performed at the Abbey Theatre in 1908, can be read retrospectively as prophetic.[11] In the play, the misunderstood hero, Thurlough, a member of a council of seven captains of the Irish army, is forced to defend his leadership on the eve of a great battle against the foreigners who have crossed the Boyne from the north. Amid accusations of treachery, he tells his accusers: 'Men, passing, see not in light of their own day the truth of their own day. So is still revered the martyr-blood that once was traitor blood.'[12]

SUPPLEMENT GIVEN AWAY WITH THE **WEEKLY FREEMAN** 22ND DECEMBER 1888.

PRICE THREE HALF-PENCE

SOON !!!

The retrospective framing of the Rising in terms of the 'blood sacrifice' of a 'failed generation' was partially rooted in an emphasis on the poetry of Joseph Mary Plunkett. Plunkett produced *The Circle and the Sword* in 1911, and a posthumous collection, *The Poems of Joseph Mary Plunkett*, was a bestseller in 1916. Delicate since childhood and sickly throughout his life, Plunkett was seriously ill when he was executed. A spiritual and troubled soul, he reflected the perpetual spectre of death in his own life and his deep religious devotion. His constant themes of suffering, death and renewal were products of his chronic ill health as much as his political convictions.[13]

The vulgarity of 'west British' or 'shoneen' tendencies among the middle classes and the popular rejection of Gaelic culture were constant themes in the Gaelic Revival. In 1903 a Gaelic League member from Youghal bemoaned to Pearse: 'In this town they seem to take no interest in the Irish language. In fact they look upon it as being vulgar and out of place. It would really disgust any person to go down to the Gaelic League rooms and see the small numbers that are studying the language of the saints and scholars.'[14] An Enniscorthy priest wrote to Pearse in 1901: '[National School] teachers are required by the Board [of Education] to have the children taught action songs in English whilst they are engaged in drilling, and such trash that the children are forced to sing is disgusting.'[15]

The Gaelic League peaked in 1908 and was declining before the formation of the Irish Volunteers. In a famous article in November 1913, Pearse announced in *An Claidheamh Soluis* that the Gaelic League was a 'spent force' and that 'the vital work to be done in the new Ireland will be done not so much by the Gaelic League itself as by men and movements that have sprung from the Gaelic League'.[16] Eoin Mac Néill's equally celebrated article, 'The North Began', called in the same paper for the establishment of a nationalist militia to counter the activities of the Ulster Volunteer Force (UVF).

The rhetoric of revolution as espoused in speeches by Volunteer leaders was dominated by allusions to Christ's resurrection. Rebirth, revival, renewal and regeneration animated republican propaganda, implying that Irish life had acquiesced in allowing British popular culture, or even worse, stage-Irish paddywhackery for the delectation of British audiences, to become seen as a legitimate expression of Irishness. Roger Casement queried: 'Is our belief in ourselves so poor that the only form our patriotism

The Pearse children (l–r): Patrick, William, Margaret and Mary Brigid.

CHARCOAL·STUDY· by
THE LATE STAFF CAPTAIN W.J.PEARSE, I.R.A.—

can take is to stand revealed as a parliamentary amusement – welcomed to pass away a jaded hour of a jaded legislature, and harmless as it is meaningless?' But he also believed that 'The wind of a new thought, the breath of a new life is already in our nostrils.'[17] The fusion of an imagined ancient idyll with modern ideas regarding social and economic progress was common in twentieth-century European nationalism: in this sense, Pearse was not an Irish mystic but a contemporary European thinker. He aligned his educational policies with the latest child-centred pedagogy, and he infused national and local values into a curriculum that was remote and alien to students.[18] Pearse assured a Philadelphia audience in 1914: 'In Ireland in recent years, we have seen again the ancient truths, have heard again the ancient voice, that we are swinging back again to the old lives, are walking the old paths, and taking up the work that had not been accomplished by those who came before us.' Previous generations had betrayed the nation through their slavish passivity in the erosion of Gaelic culture, and the task of the new generation 'rising up' was to redeem Irish nationhood: 'There has been nothing more terrible in Irish history than the failure of the last generation. Other generations have failed in Ireland, but they have failed nobly; or failing ignobly, some man among them has redeemed them from infamy by the splendour of his protest. But the failure of the last generation has been mean and shameful.'[19]

The possession and knowledge of arms was regarded as an integral part of active citizenship in the early twentieth century. The formation of the UVF, the Irish Citizen Army and the rival Irish Volunteers and National Volunteers showed that Ireland was no exception. Like his contemporaries, Pearse believed that the lack of arms in nationalist hands reflected the decline of self-respect: 'In suffering ourselves to be disarmed, acquiescing in a perpetual disarmament, neglecting every chance of arming, in sneering (as all nationalists now do), at those who have taken arms, we in effect abnegate our manhood. Unable to exercise men's rights, we do not deserve men's privileges. We are in a strict sense not fit for freedom; and freedom we shall never attain.'[20] For Pearse and others, the formation of an armed nationalist force represented an affirmation of national self-respect; drilling with arms reflected a commitment to the assertion of democratic liberty,

FACING PAGE: Charcoal drawing by William Pearse (1881–1916). Brothers William and Patrick Pearse were devoted to the theatre and viewed culture as fundamental to the political struggle for national liberation. NLI

The funeral of Jeremiah O'Donovan Rossa (1831–1915) passes along Dame Street in Dublin on 1 August 1915. For the Irish rebels of 1916, O'Donovan Rossa exemplified the Fenian refusal to moderate their demand for full Irish independence, in the face of famine, imprisonment and exile.

rather than an implicit threat to the political status quo. Many who joined the Volunteers in 1913 never believed that they would actually be called upon to fight the British Army.

Other Volunteer leaders occasionally lost patience with the high-flown rhetoric of Pearse and his comrades. In March 1916, Eoin Mac Néill scolded the Volunteer leadership: 'We have to remember that what we call our country is not a poetical abstraction, as some of us, perhaps all of us, in the exercise of our highly developed capacity for figurative thought, sometimes appear to imagine.' He went on: 'There is no such person as Caitlín Ní Houlihan or Róisín Dubh or the Sean Bhean Bhocht, who is calling upon us to serve her. What we call our country is the Irish nation, which is a concrete and visible reality.'[21]

For Roger Casement, the most cosmopolitan of Irish republican leaders, the humiliation of cultural degradation was mirrored by an abandonment of Irish manhood. In 1909 he said, 'It is a hopeless thing to think you can free Ireland when she licks her chains. She has the soul of the bastard of fear.' He excoriated the Irish Catholic as 'a poor crawling coward as a rule – afraid of his miserable soul and fearing the priest like the devil'.[22] For Joseph Mary Plunkett, the advent of the Irish Volunteers represented Ireland rising from a cultural malaise and taking its place among the modern states of western Europe:

> We, the Irish people, [are] not only reassuring our manhood, our voice and claim to stand among the nations of the world in the glorious tradition of the Christian civilisations. For a hundred and fourteen years, we have suffered the degradation consequent on our close dependency on the most degraded nation of Europe. Owing to the happy coincidence of causes, we have been able to inaugurate a movement that has put new heart into the builders of the Irish nation at the very moment when they most need encouragement, the moment when the debris has been cleared away from the foundations laid so long ago and their colossal work of reconstruction is about to begin.[23]

The level of popular support for social and political upheaval in Ireland during the opening decades of the century can be overestimated. Most nationalists remained content to exploit the opportunities provided by the

United Kingdom.[24] Although thousands of young men enjoyed Gaelic games, the majority never fully digested the ideas of Pearse or Plunkett. Knowing how to speak Irish was becoming a badge of bourgeois respectability, and the majority learning the language remained unaware of the IRB.

Royal visits to Ireland provided barometers of popular political loyalties. When Queen Victoria and Prince Albert visited in 1900, they were greeted with flags and bunting in towns and cities across Ireland.[25] Public celebrations were enthusiastic, and the donation of children's libraries to hospitals and the presentation of loyal addresses from local public authorities were central public events. The growing ambiguity of the nationalist political establishment's attitude towards these visits, however, was demonstrated by the refusal of twenty-eight of the sixty members of Dublin Corporation to welcome the Queen to Dublin. The *Irish Daily Independent* claimed that 'the Irish people as a whole shall not be supposed to be involved in such an act of self degradation. Let those who live by the union, or expect to do so, display the trappings of slaves if they please. No others ought to.'[26] Opposition to the visit was not confined to those who espoused separatism, and conservative nationalists were apathetic. W. B. Yeats castigated those involved in the public celebrations:

> Whoever is urged to pay honour to this Queen Victoria tomorrow should remember this sentence of Mirabeau's 'the silence of a people is the lesson of Kings'. She is the official head and symbol of an Empire that is robbing the South African Republic of their liberty, as it has robbed Ireland of hers. Whoever stands in the roadway cheering for Queen Victoria cheers for that Empire, dishonours Ireland and condones a crime. But whoever goes tonight to a meeting of the people and protests within the law against the welcome that unionists or time servers will have given to this English queen honours Ireland and condemns a crime.[27]

The landed gentry still dominated the judicial system in Ireland and transgressions during the visit were harshly treated. At the petty sessions in Fermanagh, a judge fined a Patrick Corr £1 for drunkenly cursing the Queen within earshot of the police: 'Cursing the Queen is downright treason. That you were drunk and cursed King William sinks into

Belfast Quaker Bulmer Hobson (1883–1969) was crucial to the reorganisation of the Irish Republican Brotherhood (IRB) in the years before the 1916 Rising. NLI

insignificance compared with the charge of cursing the Queen. Cursing the pope and King William is bad, and may stir up party feeling but cursing the Queen is one of the worst offences short of murder a man can commit. It is downright treason.'[28]

The emerging generation of advanced nationalists were set apart not by their aspirations but by their methods; after decades of stasis in the IRB, a new, serious and competent generation of activists replaced the ineffective older guard. The Dungannon Clubs was an early example of a political and cultural organisation determined to define itself by action rather than rhetoric. Founded in Belfast in 1905 by IRB members Bulmer Hobson and Denis McCullough, the society wanted to do 'some serious national work', through which 'they could control in Belfast'. The Clubs distanced itself from the merely social activities of the Irish language movement, and expressed a distinctly Ulster identity, insulated from the corrupting influence of the Dublin political establishment.[29] The movement advocated republican ideals inherited from the Volunteer movement of the eighteenth century and it attracted serious-minded recruits by promoting temperance. The organisation developed branches in towns across Ulster, recruiting members like Patrick McCartan, who later rose to prominence in Sinn Féin and the Volunteers. It issued twenty-three editions of its weekly newspaper *The Republic* between 1906 and 1907, before amalgamating with W. P. Ryan's Dublin-based *The Peasant.* The Dungannon Clubs later merged with Cumann na nGaedheal to form the Sinn Féin League in 1907.

The IRB and kindred cultural movements were selective in their use of history. The perceived degradation of national culture epitomised by the decline of the Irish language, the proliferation of English newspapers and the popularity of British popular culture fuelled the urgency to nurture a distinctly Irish popular culture. While the feats of Wolfe Tone, Robert Emmet and the Young Irelanders filled the pages of Alice Milligan and Anna Johnston's *Shan Van Vocht* and Arthur Griffith's *Sinn Féin*, the humiliation of the Great Famine of 1845 to 1852 was rarely, if ever, broached in nationalist rhetoric. James Connolly epitomised the serious tone of the new generation of activists:

If the national movement of our day is not merely to re-enact the old sad tragedies of our past history, it must show itself capable of rising to the exigencies of the moment, it must demonstrate to the people of

Copyright.]   [Published by J. J. P. O'Healy, 23 Bachelor's Walk.

Sınn Feın Abu!

Arthur Griffith (1871–1922) exemplified the conservative character of early Sinn Féin; however, his energy and persistence sustained the party through bleak times. This portrait is taken from a collection of republican postcards in the National Library of Ireland. NLI

Ireland and the world at large that nationality is not merely the morbid idealising of the past, but is capable of formulating a distinct and definite answer to the problems of the present, and a political and economic creed capable of adjustment to the wants of the future.[30]

The Boer War (1899–1902) was scrutinised closely by Irish nationalists, and the fortunes of the Boer forces provided proof, to those who sought it, that the British military was not invincible. Nationalist newspapers rejoiced in the Boers' military successes, and GAA clubs such as the Athenry De Wetts and the Tuam Krugers, named after Boer leaders, reflected the link between Gaelic games and nationalist politics. This widely reported war provided disparate branches of nationalist Ireland with a common cause, building on the renewed nationalist front that had staged the 1898 commemoration of the 1798 Rebellion. The newly united Irish Parliamentary Party displayed a cohesion not seen since the death of Parnell. Unionists cited the numbers of Irishmen fighting for the military in the conflict, but Irish Parliamentary Party MPs cheered British defeats in the House of Commons. Support for the Boer cause was espoused at meetings of the Irish Transvaal Committee. The establishment of the *United Irishman* by Arthur Griffith and William Rooney in 1899 facilitated the articulation of anti-imperialist rhetoric. Publishing the fortunes of the 'Irish brigades' under John MacBride, Arthur Lynch and John Blake, it incubated a discourse that was to become familiar in Irish politics.[31]

The exploits of Irishmen fighting against the British in South Africa were followed closely by nationalists in Ireland during the Boer War, making John MacBride (back row, far right) (1865–1916) a household name. KILMAINHAM GAOL ARCHIVE

The constitutional nationalist tradition, exemplified by Charles Stewart Parnell (1846–91), shared many ideas, supporters and sympathies with the physical-force tradition – they should not be considered wholly separate ideologies. In this picture, the chief is surrounded by party stalwarts who sought to form a lasting alliance with the Liberal Party at Westminster to further the cause of Irish independence.

At the turn of the century, most nationalists still accepted the British Empire as a concept; many shared the British colonial view of a world governed by civilised white people, set apart from barbarians and lesser breeds. Most nationalists, with the exception of an irreconcilable if toothless fringe, placidly accepted a place within the United Kingdom and the British Empire, and the anticipated Home Rule Bill promised to cement a new relationship between Britain and Ireland. National politics remained the preserve of the Irish Parliamentary Party, which anticipated Home Rule as the culmination of Ireland's political ambition. By the turn of the century, the political issues that had preoccupied Catholics – land reform, disestablishment, local government – had been remedied through parliamentary reforms that were in themselves revolutionary.[32] Since 1898, local government, in the form of county councils and urban and rural district councils, had been dominated (outside the north-east) by the United Irish League, the political grass roots of the Irish Parliamentary Party. These men regarded themselves as the natural inheritors of a Home Rule parliament, safely ensconced within the Union and the Empire, delivering the spoils of office to Catholics.

The Irish Parliamentary Party's ability to be 'all things to all men' obscured the reality that it represented disparate pressure groups and political traditions of varying hues.[33] On a political level, support for the Empire could coexist with support for Home Rule. Thomas Kettle was once active in distributing pro-Boer propaganda, argued the British Empire was based on theft, and had protested against the playing of 'God Save the King' at the Royal University of Ireland. Later, he embraced a liberal brand of imperialism, based on dominion federalism. He argued that Ireland's connection with the British Empire offered distinct advantages for the Irish Catholic middle class. He publicly called for conscription in Galway in November 1914 and was one of the few Irish MPs to fight on the Western Front. He was killed at the Battle of Ginchy in 1916.[34]

While nationalism and imperialism could coexist, so too could the constitutional and physical-force nationalist traditions. Rather than constituting fundamentally separate and distinct traditions, parliamentary and extra-parliamentary agitation historically exhibited a complicated relationship. To bolster popular support, militant and quasi-separatist language was frequently employed by Irish Parliamentary Party representatives.[35] William Duffy, MP for East Galway, imprisoned during the Land War, proclaimed his connection to the violence of the period as a badge of honour; participation in revolutionary movements could provide the springboard for political careers.[36] Ambivalence towards violence had a generational dimension: older nationalists dismissed physical force as the folly of youth – they believed the young men who espoused it would return to the bosom of constitutional nationalism as they matured.

Under John Redmond's leadership, the Irish Parliamentary Party had achieved substantial political progress. The party had a notably conservative outlook, however, in terms of social issues. It had excluded Ireland from measures benefiting the vulnerable in British society, including the Feeding of Necessitous School Children Act in 1906 and the medical provisions of the National Health Insurance Act in 1911. Redmond's appeal to reason, rather than ethnic or religious loyalties, his lack of a fanatical following, and his high-minded brand of diplomacy downplayed his leadership and political achievements in a society where politics and entertainment were entwined.[37] What Home Rule actually meant in practice and the future relationship of an Irish Parliament with Westminster were always left vague, and a carefully nurtured ambiguity preserved a unified Irish Parliamentary Party. During the later Home Rule debates, Redmond's seventy-three Westminster members functioned as a disciplined and cohesive force, and in 1912 Irish constitutional nationalism seemed poised for its greatest achievement.[38] Stephen Gwynn, a confidant of Redmond's, conceded that his leader was at times too uncharismatic to attract devotion from his followers:

> Ideally speaking, he ought to have seen to it that his party, which represented mainly the standpoint of Parnell's day, was kept in sympathy with the new young Ireland. But from the point of view of those who shared his outlook – and they were the vast majority, in Ireland and in the party – Redmond's essential limitation, as a leader, was that he lacked the magnetic qualities which produce idolatry and blind allegiance.[39]

A conservative world view also permeated the aspiring Catholic middle class in Ireland. The Catholic student elite overwhelmingly supported and expected Home Rule, and regarded themselves as a generation in professional preparation for their anticipated leadership role in an independent Ireland. The conservatism of this urban elite reflected a distinctly anglicised culture, where more militant political voices exerted little influence.[40] The principal differentiator of Irish society from the rest of the United Kingdom remained the adherence of almost three-quarters of the Irish population to Catholicism, and this religious distinctiveness reinforced Ireland's 'otherness' within the United Kingdom. By the turn of the century, the Catholic hierarchy was asserting itself ever more vigorously across many professional fields, including education, health and welfare. Catholicism occupied the core of nationalist middle-class identity, an indication of the dominant influence that the Church would expect to exercise in a Home Rule Ireland. Ireland's Catholicism attracted virulent sectarianism expressed at every level of British society, while a mix of racism and sectarianism gave Protestant 'Ulster' a favoured place within British policymaking, and dominated the British establishment's approach to its 'Irish Question'.[41]

The urban middle-class tendency to imitate aspects of English popular culture and the limited impact of the Irish-Ireland movement infuriated Yeats and the cultural revivalists. Physical-force nationalists denounced the 'West British tendencies' of young educated Catholic elites. Their obsession with respectability was encapsulated in the prevalence of Anglocentric mannerisms and accents. Douglas Hyde's 1892 'declaration of cultural independence', *The Necessity for De-Anglicising Ireland*, argued that nationalist leaders had confused politics and nationality, and had abandoned Irish civilisation as inferior.[42] Hyde sought to restore self-respect to the Irish people based on a rediscovery of indigenous culture, and rather than being the badge of a beaten culture, Gaelic culture should be promoted with pride.

Until the foundation of the Irish Transport and General Workers' Union (ITGWU) in 1909, the urban working poor were politically apathetic and Sinn Féin remained bourgeois, marginal and unimportant. The playwright Sean O'Casey believed that the working poor of Dublin lacked any cultural life, and admired James Larkin's 'bread and roses' vision of a new working class where high culture might displace the bookie, the pub and the pawnshop. O'Casey depicted the working poor as existing in a cultural wasteland: 'Their upper life was a hurried farewell to the *News of the World* on Sunday morning, and a dash to what was called the shortest Mass said in the land; and then a slow parade to the various pubs, and a wearisome wait till the pubs unveiled themselves by sliding the shutters down, and let the mass of men crowd in for refreshment.' An embittered O'Casey, who never glamorised the Dublin working class, highlighted their lack of political awareness:

> Not one of these brawny boys had ever even heard of [Arthur] Griffith or of [W. B.] Yeats. They lived their hard and boisterous life without a wish to hear their names. A good many of them had done seven years' service in the British Army, and now served on the Reserve, for sixpence a day wasn't to be sneezed at. What to them were the three Gaelic candles that light up every darkness: truth, nature, and knowledge? Three pints of porter, one after another, would light up the world for them.[43]

After the outbreak of the First World War, republicans sought to depict the police and the Irish regiments of the British military as alien forces seeking to exploit the Irish people for their own political goals, as in this anti-recruitment postcard. NLI

The STRANGER in the HOUSE

Depicting not just the British administration, but all aspects of British popular culture, as alien to the Irish people was a fundamental thrust of Irish separatism, as in this postcard entitled 'The Stranger in the House'. NLI

The ITGWU was founded by Larkin to represent the unskilled workers of Dublin. It experienced hostility from the traditionally conservative craft-based unions that constituted the Irish Congress of Trade Unions (ICTU).[44] By 1900, three-quarters of Irish trade union members were in amalgamated or British-based unions, and the British concept that labour and nationalism were contradictory was broadly accepted.[45] Between 1911 and 1915, however, labour representation in local government was established on a solid basis in Dublin and most large towns. The Labour Party was founded in 1912 by the ICTU but it was not organised in a meaningful sense until after 1916. The ICTU avoided divisive national questions that could create sectional or sectarian strife among its membership. It defended its British connections as necessary to avoid a breach with its northern members, and a closer union between Labour and the Irish Parliamentary Party was also precluded by the conservatism of the latter.[46]

The visit of King George V in 1911 was regarded as widely successful. Crowds lined the streets for his arrival at Kingstown (now Dún Laoghaire), and the Dublin United Tramway Company carried a record 340,751 passengers on the day. The royal party mingled with the Dublin poor at the Iveagh Play Centre on Francis Street, before a reception with the Catholic hierarchy in Maynooth. Young men paraded Grafton Street arm-in-arm singing 'Rule Britannia' and 'God Save the King'. The *Irish Independent* claimed that Dubliners had come out as never before to cheer 'the visible sign of their own Imperial entity', and praised the ceremonies:

> There has been no royal progress in Ireland in our memory witnessed by such mammoth crowds as those of Saturday, and no British sovereign coming to our shores has had such a reception, such a stupendous reception, as that accorded our royal visitors on Saturday. The Royal progress into the heart of our capital proved regal and glittering even beyond dreams. In some measure, it had the drama of a fairy story. For the rest it possessed such substance as all the King's horses and all the King's men could bestow. It was as dazzling as a dream and as solid as flesh and blood.[47]

The *Irish Independent*'s coverage failed to reflect the diverse voices in Irish nationalist politics within both the Irish-Ireland movement and the Irish

Parliamentary Party. Many nationalists viewed the visit with fascinated contempt, concerned that the Irish were once more prostrating themselves before a British monarch. The visit provided a focal point for small but articulate groups of advanced nationalists to register their disdain. The Dublin Municipal Council rejected the standard formality of presenting an oath of allegiance to the King: however, the Lord Mayor reneged on this commitment, agreed to present the oath and implored his colleagues to change their minds.[48] Respectable nationalists viewed proceedings with disfavour rather than hatred, and an umbrella political group called the United National Societies objected:

> So long as a National Government does not exist in Ireland, British Royal visits should not be welcomed by the people or recognised by their representatives. Expressions of welcome or gratification are therefore accepted as declarations of acquiescence in Dublin Castle government. Discountenance and repel all attempts and intrigues to represent Ireland as sinking her right of nationhood.[49]

The diverse commentary on the royal visit provides a snapshot of the formative political discourse of this period. The emphasis on national degeneration, denationalisation and moral decrepitude reflected themes that became commonplace in republican propaganda. Larkin's *The Irish Worker*, the newspaper of the ITGWU, satirised the royal address:

> Stand condemned before the nations;
> Bow your necks to foreign thrall,
> Play the knavish, base west-Briton;
> Fawn and crouch at England's call.[50]

Larkin's barbed doggerel was aimed at the barely literate poor of the Dublin slums, and his ability to communicate serious social and political doctrines through crude invective was an effective tool in mobilising his target audience. *The Irish Worker* dismissed the crowds that gathered for the royal visit: 'The crowds who stood open mouthed on our streets last week when the English king was here cared nothing for himself or the British Empire. It was the novelty of the thing that attracted them. They would stand and cheer as long and loudly, nay even louder, at a dog fight in a back lane.

Sgoil Éanna, Ráṫ Feapnáin : Iománaíoṫe (Sóipip), Luċt buaíoṫe Cupaío-míp Baile Áṫa Cliaṫ, 1910-11.
St. Enda's College, Rathfarnham : Junior Hurling Team, Holders of Dublin Schools Cup, 1910-11.
S. Ó Conċoḃaip, p. Ḃpeaṫnaċ, R. Mac Amlaoiḃ, b. Ó Tuaṫail, S. Ó Duḃġaill, S. Ó Dúnlaing, e. Mac Ḋaiḃeaċ,
C. Mac Fionnlaoiċ, U. Ó Cúlaċáin, S. Mac Diapmada (Taoipeaċ), b. Seoiġe, U. Ó Tuaṫail, T. Ó hOipín,
S. Ó hOipín, S. Paop.

ABOVE: St Enda's hurling team, 1910–11. Gaelic games represented an alternative to soccer for working-class boys, and to cricket and rugby for the middle classes. They were an important expression of nationalist sentiment. NLI

BELOW: St Enda's School Theatre Group *c.* 1910. The boys of St Enda's were encouraged to explore national history and literature through theatre and song. PEARSE MUSEUM

There is no real loyalty to the King in the country, and very little in England.'[51] It also made the wider political point:

> The welfare of the people of Ireland is more important to us than the smiles of King or Queen. While there is a hungry man, woman or child in Ireland, while there is even one of our people ill-clad, or ill-treated, we will join in no display of hypocritical loyalty. While there is a barefooted child in this country we cannot afford to buy flags or fireworks, nor present loyal addresses. We will demand, and if necessary fight, for what we consider are our rights; we ask no favours. Because we consider 'loyalty' dangerous to our class, we are out to make rebels. [52]

The visit generated a scathing pamphlet by the minuscule Dublin branch of the Socialist Party of Ireland, highlighting the anti-democratic and elitist nature of the proceedings:

> A people mentally poisoned by the adulation of royalty can never attain to that spirit of self-reliant democracy necessary for the attainment of social freedom. The mind accustomed to political kings can easily be reconciled to social kings – capitalist kings of the workshop, the mill, the railway, the ships and the docks. Thus, coronations and kings visits are by our astute, never sleeping masters made into huge imperialist propagandist campaigns in favour of political and social schemes against democracy.[53]

Arthur Griffith formed Cumann na nGaedheal in 1900 from a motley group of loosely associated literary and political organisations. The movement promoted de-anglicisation, with a primary emphasis on cultural activities. Major John MacBride, Maud Gonne and William Rooney were founding members and the organisation subsequently amalgamated with the National Council (formed in 1903 to protest against the royal visit) and the Dungannon Clubs to form the Sinn Féin party.[54] All three organisations represented non-violent cultural or political movements, although IRB members were certainly present in all of them. Griffith combined cultural commentary with economic policy in his *Sinn Féin* newspaper. His emphasis on the resurgence of national self-respect, and contempt for the subservience of the previous decades, reflected the contemporary republican discourse on cultural and political renewal:

> We have no sympathy with the pessimists who at times like this speak as if Ireland had lost her spirit. Ireland has never in a century shown a more self respecting spirit than she does now. In the nineteenth century she bent her head to every British Monarch's visit. In this century she has bent to none. However much slavishness is left in Ireland today, it is in manhood far ahead of the Ireland that sprawled before George IV and welcomed Victoria when she came triumphing over a land whose peasants were dying of famine. Our eyes today see as national faults and defect things that in the past we regarded as harmless or even virtuous. That is why some of us, forgetting to make comparisons of now and then, yield to the false belief that we are receding rather than advancing. Ireland is advancing. Her people have diminished in numbers but they have strengthened in character and the flabby old Ireland that danced in the Castle yard is as dead as Queen Victoria.[55]

The IRB's newspaper, *Irish Freedom*, was predictably visceral in its contempt for the royal visit: 'We scorn and spit upon the Empire, an empire built on blood and desolation; we shall never remain in it willingly; we want none of its spoils and we repudiate its atrocities; we will not sell our birthright.' The IRB, 'in the face of hog, dog, or devil', stood 'for Ireland, not for Ireland's portion of any Empire, not for an Ireland in swaddling clothes and leading strings, but for a self-reliant free Ireland'.[56] Popular support for the IRB in the years preceding the Rising was negligible. Activist Diarmuid Lynch believed that 'there may not have been in a whole district a single man imbued with republican ideals'. In 1911 the IRB mustered 1,500 members and 'only an odd man here and there belonged to an active circle'.[57] The revitalisation of the IRB was undertaken by Bulmer Hobson, Patrick McCartan and Denis McCullough, who culled older, quiescent members and replaced them with younger militants.[58] This northern-based group wrested control of the IRB from its Dublin-based leaders, P. T. Daly, Fred Allan and Sean O'Hanlon, who were blamed for letting the movement descend into a glorified drinking club. The veteran Fenian Tom Clarke arrived back in Dublin from the United States in 1907 and he proved an inspirational figure. The appointment of Seán Mac Diarmada (a young west Belfast barman) as a full-time organiser signalled that a new, more militant phase had begun.

Despite the alliance between the Irish Parliamentary Party and the Liberals at Westminster, racial and religious prejudice perennially characterised English attitudes towards Ireland.[59] The British constitutional crisis of 1910–11 paved the way for Home Rule, as the power of the House of Lords to block legislation indefinitely was reduced to two years. The Liberal Party resented being held hostage to Redmond's demands, however, and the passing of the Home Rule Bill concealed the mutual distrust that plagued Anglo-Irish relationships. By legislating in 1912, Prime Minister Asquith ended an enduring source of instability in British politics. Both the Liberals and the Conservatives supported the exclusion of the north-east of Ireland from Home Rule.

Despite reassurances that the Protestant unionist majority in Ulster would be excluded from any settlement, drilling by unionist clubs commenced in 1912. Unionist clubs were formed in April 1911 as a focus for popular opposition to Home Rule, and there were 164 clubs pledged to maintaining the union by the end of the year.[60] The UVF, which was formed in January 1913, established a five-man provisional government, and by early 1914, 110,000 Protestants were drilling across the nine northern counties. Although he knew that Home Rule would not be forced on Ulster, Edward Carson led an impressive unionist movement that successfully harnessed the support of all sections of Protestant society, while openly pledging armed resistance against the British state. The toleration (and even admiration and active support) of Carson and the paramilitary UVF by the political and military elite in Britain exposed double standards.

The First World War and Popular Politics

Local government was devolved in Ireland in 1898 and the establishment of town, rural and urban district councils swept away the last vestiges of landlord involvement in civil administration.[61] For most nationalists, participation in politics involved membership of their United Irish League branch. Issues such as striking the annual rates for property owners, lobbying for the sale of landed estates to the state for redistribution among tenant farmers, the building of labourers' cottages, and the provision of public sanitation occupied the energies of local bodies, incubating democracy at a grass-roots level. Irish MPs spent considerable time in London and many had little connection with their constituencies. Involvement in constituency issues varied between members, but representatives saw their primary function as legislating, and local issues were left to party activists.[62] Local politics tended to be colourful, and public meetings and political contests were boisterous affairs, characterised by a lively mixture of humour and invective.[63] Local politics was covered by partisan newspaper editors, and political speeches and council meetings were exhaustively reported, often with scant regard for libel laws.

The year 1914 witnessed pivotal developments that transformed nationalist Ireland, invigorated the physical-force tradition and ultimately destroyed the Irish Parliamentary Party. One of the many unforeseen casualties of the First World War, John Redmond's party was a victim of its own support for the war effort. The outbreak of conflict in 1914, coupled with the militant resistance of northern unionists to the Home Rule Bill, created conditions in which militant movements gained a hitherto unthinkable popular credibility. The granting of Home Rule seemed a formality in 1912 and that in itself undermined the Irish Parliamentary Party's *raison d'être*, while the war years witnessed the erosion of support for the party among an increasingly sceptical population. As an unpopular and futile war dragged on interminably, and a British war cabinet dominated by unionists sidelined Home Rule, party members concluded that Redmond had been hoodwinked.

In retrospect, Redmond's enthusiasm for the war was a strategic error. His willingness to commit young Irish lives to the battlefield of Europe should be understood within its contemporary context. In the early twentieth century, Irish nationalism was unencumbered by defining ideological or doctrinal parameters, and it was accordingly free to straddle a surprisingly broad spectrum of loyalties, identities and social classes. Redmond's stubborn belief that Catholic Ireland should play a full role in the British Empire, his unwavering commitment to the Allied cause (which claimed the life of his brother William) and his early concession that partition was inevitable reflected the defining pragmatism of mainstream nationalist politics.[64] Like other political leaders, he assumed that the war would be a brief affair and that Catholic Ireland's participation would nullify Carson's enthusiastic warmongering, demonstrating the maturity of Irish nationalism with dedicated Irish soldiers fighting for a just British cause.

Despite the changed conditions generated by the war, the 1916 Rebellion and the subsequent transformation of politics were far from inevitable. Nationalist political discourse lacked internal debate, owing to consensus on the national question and overwhelming approval of the tactics and leadership of the Irish Parliamentary Party. The demands of the IPP for Home Rule were couched in the language of moderation and 'common sense', as Redmond explained in 1910: 'What Ireland wants is really so reasonable, so moderate, so commonplace, in view of the experience of the nations, and especially of the British Empire, that once it is understood, all the fears and arguments of honest opponents must vanish into thin air.'[65]

Sinn Féin, founded in 1907, remained a small and ill-defined organisation that did not contest parliamentary elections, except for a single one in north Leitrim in 1907 when its candidate failed on an abstentionist ticket.[66] In a political atmosphere defined by consensus, moderation and deference, Sinn Féin's radicalism alienated wider opinion, and republican opposition to constitutionalism remained diffuse. Arthur Griffith, Sinn Féin's driving force, conceived of his organisation as an intellectual pressure group rather than as an electoral party. The *United Irishman* and *Sinn Féin* newspapers, edited and largely written by Griffith himself, advocated abstentionism from Westminster and an independent Irish state under a dual monarchy. Griffith focused primarily on the achievement of Irish independence through political means, with a pragmatic emphasis on taxation, industrial growth and social housing. Griffith's thought had a closer political affinity with the Home Rule leadership than the more assertive tendencies within the Gaelic League movement, with which Sinn Féin was often associated.[67] For most Irish separatists, Sinn Féin remained a Dublin-based fringe movement, removed from the reality of people's daily lives, until after the 1916 Rebellion.

For the small ardent community of militant radicals, Ireland's political life during this period was bogged down in a mire of constitutional compromise. Éamonn Ceannt (later a member of the secret committee that

The Officers and Executive of Cumann na mBan

invite your attendance to their

CONVENTION CEILIDH

At 25 PARNELL SQUARE

On SUNDAY, 31st OCTOBER, 1915
(oroče samna).

P. Mahon, Printer, Dublin.

Founded in April 1914, Cumann na mBan ('The Women's Organisation') sought to provide 'authentic Irish' forms of entertainment, such as this *céilidh*, for its members, thus avoiding the moral danger of becoming a soldier's 'moll' or girlfriend. NLI

Drawing of an angel by one of the Pearse brothers – most likely William. The Pearse family ran an ecclesiastical sculpture business, reinforcing Patrick Pearse's personal commitment to sacrifice and his belief in the centrality of national 'resurrection'. NLI

planned the insurrection) told an audience in 1912: 'Ireland has abandoned her claim to nationhood and is willing, nay anxious, to take her part in the Empire on which the sun never sets. She is anxious to enjoy the loot obtained by England in her foreign wars. She will calmly assist in crushing those nations such as the Egyptians and the Indians which have the impertinence to harbour thoughts of nationhood in their heathen hearts'.[68]

Partly to counteract what it regarded as the 'shoneenism' of Irish culture, Sinn Féin advocated the independence of the Irish nation and sought to secure international recognition for an independent Irish Republic. The party promoted non-violent protest, a dual monarchy, a protective system for Irish industries and commerce, a national civil service, and educational reform ('to render its basis national and industrial by the compulsory teaching of the Irish language and Irish history'[69]). The British parliament at Westminster was rejected as 'treasonable to our national demand', as the 'strength of Ireland's sons is contact with the motherland, divorce from it means defeat'.[70]

By its own admission, Sinn Féin was popularly dismissed before 1916 as 'unpractical visionaries and mere literary doctrinaires, cranks, factionalists, soreheads or worse'.[71] The party made no impact outside of Dublin and its reform agenda never penetrated the popular consciousness of rural people. Rather than providing a radical alternative, Sinn Féin's political demands mirrored those of their constitutional rivals in the United Irish League (UIL); while there were political differences, they were minimal. The UIL's objectives included full national self-government, abolition of landlordism, provision of cottages for agricultural labourers and 'the preservation of the Gaelic language as part of the struggle for the recovery of our national freedom'.[72] The UIL's social policies to protect the rural poor were more sophisticated than Sinn Féin's, whose first constitution ignored landlordism, agricultural labourers, economic distress and educational inequality.[73]

The startling parade of events from 1914 to 1921 shattered nationalist Ireland's illusions about the unchallenged primacy of the constitutional tradition and the rejection of political violence as illegitimate. The new thinking regarding national rights and entitlements brought previously unpopular notions of Irish sovereignty within the theoretical framework of submerged European minorities. For nationalists in Ireland, the British establishment's argument that the Allies were acting 'in defence of small nations' made their denial of Irish sovereignty increasingly irrational, reinforcing a renewed sense of nationalist solidarity.[74]

The rise of the UVF, an armed unionist militia formed to resist Home Rule by force, was a momentous development. Resistance to Home Rule was eminently predictable but few foresaw the willingness of elements of the British political establishment, notably the Tory party, not only to play the 'Orange card' but actively to countenance violent resistance.[75] The formation of the UVF represented a new departure in Irish affairs. The more perceptive nationalist leaders realised that a new political dynamic could be created in response to unionist provocation. Bulmer Hobson (a founding member of the Irish Volunteers) recalled that the IRB had 'decided that the time had come to start the Volunteers, but that the IRB must not show its hand. We were looking around for a respected figure who would become the focal point of a public movement, when an article entitled "The North Began", which appeared in *An Claidheamh Soluis*, the official organ of the Gaelic League, on 1 November 1913, provided us with the necessary opening.'

Eoin Mac Néill, who wrote the article, was a leading intellectual in the Irish-Ireland movement, spearheading respectable, secular, educated and moderate nationalist opinion.[76] He wrote:

> It is evident that the only solution now possible is for the empire either to make terms with Ireland or to let Ireland go her own way. In any case, it is manifest that all Irish people, Unionist as well as nationalist, are determined to have their own way in Ireland. On that point, and it is the main point, Ireland is united. It is not to follow, and it will not follow, that any part of Ireland, majority or minority, is to interfere with the liberty of any other part. Sir Edward Carson may yet, at the head of his Volunteers, 'march to Cork'. If so, their progress will probably be accompanied by the greetings of ten times their number of National Volunteers, and Cork will give them a hospitable and a memorable reception.[77]

Having secured the cooperation of Mac Néill and The O'Rahilly (manager of the Gaelic League's periodical, *An Claidheamh Soluis*), a small group of hardened conspirators, including Patrick Pearse, Seán Mac Diarmada, Éamonn Ceannt and Piaras Béaslaí, consented in September 1913 to the formation of a provisional committee to direct a new popular body of nationalist Volunteers.[78] Invitations were issued to nationalist organisations in advance of the inaugural public meeting, requesting sympathetic groups to publicise the new force. Their provisional constitution outlined the Volunteers' aims as 'to secure and maintain the rights and liberties common to all the people of Ireland, to train, discipline, arm and equip a body of Volunteers for the above purpose, and to unite for this purpose Irishmen of every creed and of every party and class'.[79] Mac Néill assured their first public meeting at the Rotunda in Dublin on 25 November: 'If ever in history a people could say that an opportunity was given them by God's Will to make an honest and manly stand for their rights, that opportunity is given us today.'[80] The meeting proved a success; Hobson's estimate of 7,000 in attendance seems exaggerated but nearby streets were indeed blocked by crowds clamouring to get into the building. Although the new movement's committee was dominated by IRB members, there was no formal IRB control. Of the first provisional committee of thirty members, twelve were members of the IRB, along with four from the United Irish League, four from the Ancient Order of Hibernians and ten unaffiliated to any other organisation.[81]

The Irish Volunteers were not merely an IRB front and the vast majority of Volunteers were not members of the brotherhood. A small cadre within the IRB, however, sought to control the movement. Of the seven eventual members of the self-appointed military council that planned the insurrection, Éamonn Ceannt, Joseph Plunkett, Thomas MacDonagh and Patrick Pearse held positions on the Volunteer executive and on the Dublin brigade staff, but Séan Mac Diarmada and Tom Clarke were not Volunteer officers, and James Connolly was not a member of the IRB or the Irish Volunteers. This group, along with a coterie of talented organisers such as Piaras Béaslaí, Liam Mellows, Michael Collins and Edward Daly, manipulated the Volunteers for their own ends. Mac Néill's prominence at the head of the organisation served as camouflage. Some prominent

INCORPORATED UNDER THE LAWS OF THE
STATE OF NEW YORK

NUMBER 33

SHARES 20

THE GAELIC AMERICAN PUBLISHING COMPANY

Capital Stock, $25,000

This is to Certify that *John Devoy* is the owner of *twenty* Shares of the Capital Stock of

The Gaelic American Publishing Company

transferable only on the books of the Company by the holder hereof in person or by duly authorized Attorney upon surrender of this Certificate properly endorsed.

In Witness Whereof this Certificate has been prepared by the Directors and the said corporation has caused the same to be signed by its duly authorized officers and to be sealed with the seal of the corporation this *fifteenth* day of *July* A.D. 190*3*.

Thos. J. O'Sullivan
Treasurer.

Daniel F. Cohalan
President.

← Full Paid and Non-Assessable →

$5 SHARES EACH

ABOVE (l–r): Roger Casement (1864–1916) and John Devoy (1842–1928). Devoy was fundamental to the fortunes of Irish rebels by raising large sums of cash and generating political support in the US.

BELOW: A voluntary subscription to John Devoy's New York-based newspaper, the *Gaelic American* – a key means of fundraising in Irish-American political circles. NLI

Ancient Order of Hibernians in America

NATIONAL OFFICERS

JAMES J. REGAN, President · St. Paul, Minn.

JOSEPH McLAUGHLIN, Vice Pres. - Phila., Pa.

JAMES T. McGINNIS, Secretary, - Scranton, Pa.

HON. T. H. MALONEY, Treas., Council Bluffs, Ia.

NATIONAL DIRECTORS

REV. WM. T. McLAUGHLIN - Union Hill, N. J.

PATRICK T. MORAN · · Washington, D. C.

CHARLES J. FOY · · · Perth, Ont., Canada

MICHAEL F. POWERS, · Grand Rapids, Mich.

WILLIAM J. DOHERTY · · · · Chicago, Ill.

RIGHT REV. JOHN P. CARROLL, Bishop of Helena, Montana, Chaplain

OFFICE OF
PATRICK T. MORAN, Nat'l Director
3259-3261 M STREET

OFFICE OF
NATIONAL PRESIDENT

Ladies' Auxiliary, Ancient Order of Hibernians
OF AMERICA

RIGHT REV. D. J. O'CONNELL, National Chaplain
Richmond, Va.

Motto: Friendship, Unity and Christian Charity

NATIONAL OFFICERS

MRS. MARY F. McWHORTER, President
1021 E. 46th Street, Chicago, Ill.

MRS. ADELIA CHRISTY, Vice-President
7603 Decker Avenue, Cleveland, Ohio

MRS. SUSAN M. McNAMEE, Secretary
372 Main Street, Medford, Mass.

MISS MARGARET McQUADE, Treasurer
2223 Murray Avenue, Pittsburgh, Pa.

NATIONAL DIRECTORS

MRS. SARAH J. ROBINSON, National Director
3007 E. Main Street, Richmond, Va.

MRS. MARY ARTHUR, National Director
1924 Park Street, Indianapolis, Ind.

MISS ADA K. GANNON,
National Chairman Irish History
217 E. 10th Street, Davenport, Iowa

MRS. ELLEN RYAN JOLLY, Chairman of the "Monument to the Nuns of the Battlefield," 159 West Ave., Pawtucket, R. I.

The Ancient Order of Hibernians was a Catholic fraternal organisation that promoted the interests of Irish Catholics in the United States. Its role in promoting the ideals of the Irish rebels was crucial to generating funds and support across the US.

Volunteers, including Mac Néill, Bulmer Hobson, Michael O'Rahilly and J.J. 'Ginger' O'Connell, were distrusted by the conspirators and kept in the dark about the secret military council's plans until shortly before the Rising. To these men, the actions of the secret military council were a betrayal of the Volunteers at the behest of an unelected cabal of conspirators.

To the average observer, there was little that was obviously conspiratorial about the Irish Volunteers. Young men were trained in drill, often by British Army veterans or reservists, with route marches usually held at weekends. Officers in local companies were elected by the members themselves and aspiring Volunteers had to commit their free time and disposable income, as uniforms and equipment had to be purchased from one's own resources.[82] Most Volunteers rarely got to handle a rifle, or to purchase a uniform, and many new recruits soon tired of the tedium. The motivations of young members ranged from circumventing parental control, to adventure seeking and ideological conviction. Most members believed that a trained body of men represented a warning against any attempt by the British government to abdicate its responsibilities to the nationalist community: by joining the movement, they were actively defending the right of Ireland to self-government.

In the face of mass unionist mobilisation, the Irish Volunteers made little headway and nationalists in the north remained passive. RIC Inspector General Neville Chamberlain was unconcerned about nationalist mobilisation: 'the proposal to form an Irish Volunteer corp in support of the nationalist demand for self-government has made little tangible progress'. The movement, Chamberlain reported, 'is still advocated by extremists but is not expected to develop to any extent so long as the Home Rule Bill is in suspense, unless it receives encouragement from the Irish Party'. The Ancient Order of Hibernians, Sinn Féin and the IRB 'each have a member-ship in certain districts, but at present, their influence is unimportant'. [83]

In the early months of their existence, the Irish Volunteers lacked political and military credibility until their opponents in the Irish Parliamentary Party began to see merit in enhancing their own political credibility by wielding a popular militia against the British establishment. A hostile takeover of the Irish Volunteers by Redmond's party in May 1914 saw the movement's political direction become inherently linked to the course of the First World War, and the original character and purpose of the organisation evaporated. The takeover of the movement involved local members of the United Irish League establishing new branches of the Volunteers, or flooding existing ones with new members. The nationalist takeover changed the social character of the organisation, as an older, more respectable leadership was established that owed its loyalty to the political leadership of John Redmond. The unprecedented growth of the movement in the summer of 1914 resulted in the immediate loss of authority by the cabal of IRB conspirators who had successfully captured key positions.

The reaction of the RIC to the Volunteers initially ranged from bemusement to contempt, and the militia was treated with a lack of seriousness by the authorities. The RIC was tasked with monitoring the Volunteers' activities, openly following companies on their marches, watching their drill practice and attending their meetings. Members' names and details were assiduously compiled and this knowledge reflected the relatively public nature of their activities. Membership of the movement appealed primarily to the working and lower-middle classes, and police reports invariably stressed the youthful nature of companies and their apparent 'lack of substance'. Terms such as 'cornerboys', 'clerks', 'boys' and 'strawmen' were employed in descriptions of the membership in police reports that emphasised the absence of 'those with a stake in the country'. In rural areas, companies attracted farmers' sons, farm labourers and those free of familial or professional responsibility.

Throughout 1913 and 1914, the authorities in Ireland were preoccupied with the rise of the Ulster Volunteers and little consideration was given to the rival nationalist militias. In January 1914, Chamberlain, the Inspector General of the RIC, reported to his superiors that 'the situation in Ulster appears to grow more serious as time advances' and that 17,000 rifles were in the hands of the UVF in the province.[84] At the beginning of the year, Protestant football clubs in Belfast stopped playing matches so that their members could concentrate on activities connected with the UVF. The police estimated that there were 4,000 rifles in Protestant hands in the city. Counties with significant Protestant minorities experienced a change in the political atmosphere and in County Donegal, where the UVF had 2,700 members, the police reported the anti-Home Rule agitation 'has led to strained relations between unionists and nationalists'. Branches of the UVF were formed in rural districts with small Protestant populations: four branches were active in County Leitrim and a general inspection was carried out at Killegar.[85]

The annual Orange celebrations took place in Belfast in July 1914 and marches attracted the largest crowds in decades. Chamberlain reported that 'an uneasy restless feeling' prevailed in the city, as 18,000 members of the Orange Order marched, while the small force of Irish National Volunteers could muster only 2,100 men. The atmosphere was tense across the province and, in Cavan, tension reached levels not witnessed in decades, with the police reporting that 'from a political and sectarian point of view the outlook is dangerous'. Members of the UVF drilling in the county totalled 3,461, alongside 6,366 members of the Irish National Volunteers.[86]

Police figures attest to the rapid growth of the National Volunteers during the summer of 1914. In July, there were 7,888 members drilling in Limerick, 10,215 in Donegal and 7,630 in Down. A few short months after the Irish Parliamentary Party took over the movement, the organisation had a combined strength of 60,000 men in the nine Ulster counties alone, but it remained 'very deficient in arms and organisation'.[87] For the first time, social and political elites were becoming associated with the movement, marking a change from its previous 'disrespectable' character. Chamberlain reported that 'The Irish Volunteer movement has spread over the whole country. Persons of superior class have joined, and the police report a general eagerness on the part of the members to possess arms.' While still chronically short of arms and ammunition, the Volunteers managed to land arms at Howth in July. The Inspector General reported that it 'at once gave a great stimulus to the Volunteer movement'. However, Chamberlain concluded that 'it was manifest that the sympathies of the Irish Volunteers in the prospect of war with Germany were on the side of England'.

The force now had its highest numbers, with 160,000 members nationwide, and the Inspector General of the RIC noted the moderating influence of the Volunteers' new leadership:

> The Irish American Alliance, Sinn Fein and IRB possess very little influence throughout the country, evidenced by the fact that although the original promotors [sic] of the Volunteer movement were to a considerable extent representative of the extreme party, the governing council as well as the membership of the force is now overwhelmingly in accord with the policy of Mr John Redmond.88

Despite the formation of the UVF and the Irish National Volunteers, few contemporaries anticipated violent political upheaval in the years preceding the Rising. *The Irish Volunteer* claimed in 1915 that 'Ireland has been restored to as normal a state of good health as a country under the rule of external force can expect to have. For some time back, she has been living in a state of stupor, stupefied by liberalism, doles, jobs, and trust in British democracy.'[89] In early 1916, James Connolly excoriated the political stasis into which Ireland had descended: 'In August 1914, it seemed to many of the most hopeful of us that Ireland had at length taken its final plunge into the abyss of Imperialism and bade a long farewell to all hopes of a separate unfettered existence as a nation.'[90]

The sudden emergence of the physical-force tradition and of a fundamentally new political conception of Irish nationalism necessitated the destruction of constitutional nationalism. The bitterness and hostility generated by this demolition has been underestimated. The Irish Parliamentary Party's enthusiasm for the war effort undermined its local credibility, sapped the morale of its members and discredited its leader's political judgment, placing it increasingly at odds with ordinary Irish people. The focus on recruitment meetings left nationalists disillusioned with conventional constitutional politics. Redmondites misjudged the popular mood of anger, dismissing it as the natural deviance of the young, the ignorant and the poor. The Irish Volunteers confronted the paternal leadership of older nationalists in a conspicuous display of lack of deference towards established political conventions.

Pro-British sentiment among Catholics was generally passive rather than active. IRB member P. S. O'Hegarty recalled that although nationalists 'felt that England was right in the War, they did not feel that they were called upon to do anything in the way of helping England otherwise than by feeding her'.[91] The British war effort was bolstered by a formidable propaganda onslaught in Ireland. This wrong-footed the IRB, as denigrating militarism could be portrayed as cowardice. In August 1913, 20,780 Irishmen were serving in the British Army. Following the outbreak of the First World War, 17,804 reservists and 12,462 special reservists rejoined, making a total mobilisation of 51,046 Irishmen in British uniforms. After the outbreak of the conflict, three new divisions were established – the 10th, the 16th and the 36th – consisting of twelve battalions each. Added to the original sixteen Irish battalions of the regular forces, this totalled fifty-two Irish battalions. By October 1915, enlistment since the war commenced had reached 75,293 – a cumulative total of 126,339 recruits. An average weekly supply of 1,100 recruits was required to maintain army reserves at an adequate level: while the Irish recruits in the first year of the conflict exceeded these figures, the numbers collapsed by autumn 1915. In October, a new Department of Recruiting was organised, with provincial directors, county controllers and local committees. There were 416,409 unmarried men of military age in Ireland in August 1915, of whom 252,000 were involved in agriculture. The military reported that 'only a small response has attended recruiting efforts' in the agricultural sector, and that other sectors 'from which in the main the recruits have been drawn,

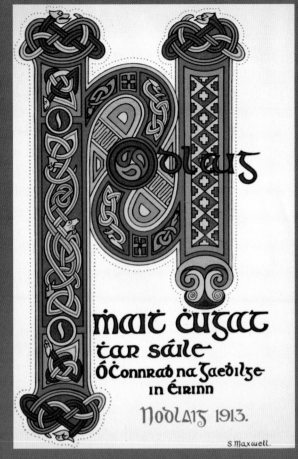

RIGHT: A Gaelic League Christmas card. The Gaelic League sought to promote 'authentic' expressions of Gaelic culture in place of popular British cultural motifs. NLI

BELOW: A Christmas card sent to Patrick Pearse in 1915. The image was typical of the motifs employed by the Gaelic League in promoting traditional Irish crafts. NLI

are not in a position to provide an additional large contingent of recruits'. By December 1915, Ulster had provided the most recruits at 49,760, followed by Leinster at 27,458, with Munster at 14,190 and Connacht at a mere 3,589. The recruiting authorities excused their failure as being due to the reliance of agriculture on manpower.[92] Farmers had done well from a boom in wartime prices; an increase of over £4 million in Irish banks in the second half of 1914 attested to the increased revenues. Deposits continued at an extraordinary level during the conflict, reaching £6.4 million for 1916 and £15.4 million for 1917.[93]

Conclusion

The strategy of the leaders of the 1916 Rebellion reflected a logical and brutal series of calculations. The Rising represented more than the irrationalism of a small group of intellectuals, or a manifestation of economic grievance. Hatred of England did not inspire the small cadre who planned the Rebellion; it was instead a repudiation of the cultural and spiritual desolation wrought by the empire and the humiliation that it imposed on its subjects. George Russell recognised that empires humiliate native culture, and the Rising represented for him 'a plea for spirit as against dull matter, for imagination against empiricism'.[94] The 1916 Rising took place during the most destructive war in human history to date and Irish revolutionaries were not immune to the European intellectual culture that promoted violent expressions of national self-respect.

In the aftermath of the Rebellion, novelist James Stephens wrote: 'We might have crept into liberty like some kind of domesticated man, whereas now we may be allowed to march into freedom with the honours of war.'[95] The new revolutionaries differed from previous generations in the seriousness of their intent, and the political climate generated by the foundation of the UVF and the outbreak of war offered them an unprecedented opportunity. For the conspirators, the Rising had to restore an invigorating sense of popular dignity to their movement by demonstrating that Irish republicans were committed to, and capable of, concerted military action.

The sympathetic public reaction to the execution of the leaders, allied to the collapse of the Irish Parliamentary Party, facilitated previously unthinkable political possibilities. The Rising forced the original Sinn Féin to adjust to the new dynamics of Irish republicanism. By late 1917, Volunteer leaders realised that the small Sinn Féin party could be successfully reinvented as a popular movement by harnessing the anger generated by the war. For republicans to achieve a new Ireland, the creation of a broadly based political party was a prerequisite in order to establish their relevance and to strengthen their appeal. Sinn Féin benefited from devotion to an abstract concept of Irish freedom, an inherently ill-defined vision of a new Ireland that was intentionally left open to wide inter-pretation. The party's expansion after 1916 happened so quickly that woolliness became its defining characteristic, as it absorbed diverse social groups and political organisations.[96]

For ordinary nationalists, Sinn Féin represented a new beginning, appealing especially to younger idealists previously shut out of a political culture dominated by old men. Following the Rising, a young revolutionary, John Moynihan, wrote: 'The old problems have been swept rudely into the background, if not out of existence altogether; the old ways of thinking have been changed. Ireland is no longer the island of six, of four, weeks ago; the political attitude of our people has radically altered, their passivity in the hands of politicians has passed, and I hope forever.'[97]

2
PRELUDE:
THE GATHERING STORM

That woman's days were spent
In ignorant good-will,
Her nights in argument
Until her voice grew shrill.
What voice more sweet than hers
When, young and beautiful,
She rode to harriers?
This man had kept a school
And rode our wingèd horse;
This other his helper and friend
Was coming into his force;
He might have won fame in the end,
So sensitive his nature seemed,
So daring and sweet his thought.
This other man I had dreamed
A drunken, vainglorious lout.
He had done most bitter wrong
To some who are near my heart,
Yet I number him in the song;
He, too, has resigned his part
In the casual comedy;
He, too, has been changed in his turn,
Transformed utterly:
A terrible beauty is born.

'Easter, 1916' | W. B. Yeats | 25 September 1916

The Irish Volunteers

Details of the plans for the 1916 Rising were shrouded in impenetrable secrecy and confined to a handful of conspirators. The lessons of previous failed rebellions weighed heavily on the conspirators' minds. It should also be noted that the secret 'military council' that planned the Rebellion did not have full control over the Volunteers and their plans had to be hidden from senior officers, including Eoin Mac Néill. Planning for the Rising commenced in mid-September 1914, but firm details regarding the date were not decided until late 1915.[1]

The founding of the Irish Republican Brotherhood (IRB) in 1858 by James Stephens represented the determination of Irish Americans to fund a revolutionary movement at home that would make Ireland an independent republic.[2] Much of the impetus for this new society came from the Irish-American community in the north-eastern cities of the United States. Stephens' endeavours were financed by Irish exiles, including former Young Irelanders, who hoped to raise and train a volunteer militia that would return to Ireland.[3] The result was the Fenian brotherhood, an oath-bound secret society dedicated to revolution in Ireland. The brotherhood spread rapidly among Irish Americans and raised funds for the IRB through the sale of bonds. The Fenian brotherhood was succeeded by Clan na Gael in 1867, following a damaging split among the American Fenians. Clan na Gael continued the work of the brotherhood, sending funds to Ireland to support the IRB and providing arms and resources in the period preceding the Rising.

The heyday of the IRB was in the 1880s and 1890s when it played a significant role in popular land agitation, as well as infiltrating political and cultural movements, including the Land League and even the Irish Parliamentary Party. A controversial dynamite campaign in Britain in the 1880s brought the movement under unprecedented police scrutiny. By the early 1900s, the IRB was dwindling into a moribund organisation, serving more as a social club for veterans and former prisoners than as a revolutionary force.[4]

Until 1911, the Supreme Council of the IRB was largely controlled by Dublin-based activists Fred Allan, P. T. Daly and Jack O'Hanlon.[5] Allan's control of the IRB was resented by a younger, more dynamic group, which centred around the veteran Tom Clarke and included Seán Mac Diarmada,

Denis McCullough, P. S. O'Hegarty, Bulmer Hobson and Patrick McCartan. This northern-based group believed that the older leaders 'stifled all activity', and sought to seize control from them of the moribund organisation. Hobson explained, 'the conflict was the recurring one between an older generation who wished to go slowly and quietly and the younger generation who wished to get things done'.[6] Hobson, McCullough and McCartan weeded out older, less motivated members. Veteran Fenian George Lyons recalled that 'the old men in the IRB were gradually replaced by the recruitment from the young men who were noted for their sobriety and enthusiasm'.[7]

The outbreak of the First World War in July 1914 transformed the political situation in Ireland: Home Rule was shelved for the duration of the conflict, thus averting the potential for civil unrest in the north-east; large numbers of the UVF joined the British war effort and its provocative military displays came to an end; nationalist and unionist leaders found common political ground in their support for the Allies; and nationalists enlisted in the British Army, with the Irish National Volunteers splitting into rival factions over John Redmond's offer to support the British war effort.

The Ulster Volunteer Force (UVF) was founded in 1912 to resist Home Rule being imposed in the north-east of Ireland. In this image, Edward Carson (1854–1935), leader of the Irish Unionist Alliance *(centre)*, reviews a parade of the UVF. NLI

The UVF was considerably better armed and funded than the Irish Volunteers, and, as this image shows, possessed far more modern weaponry. NLI

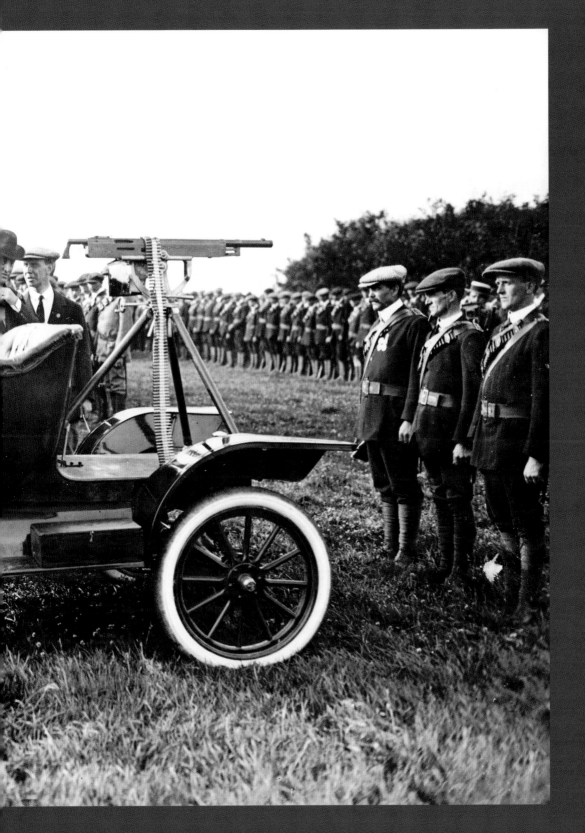

ABOVE: Edward Carson *(centre)*, a native Dubliner, was a somewhat unlikely leader of Ulster unionism. He enjoyed a brilliant legal career before devoting his energies to politics.

RIGHT: The Irish Unionist Alliance held public meetings across Ireland in the two years before the outbreak of the First World War in 1914. This card featuring Bonar Law *(left)* and Edward Carson *(right)* was distributed in advance of a major meeting held in Dublin in 1913.

The IRB was determined to manipulate the Volunteers and foment rebellion before the conclusion of the war in Europe. The Volunteers, however, languished in relative obscurity until the organisation was officially endorsed by John Redmond's Irish Parliamentary Party in May 1914. For the founders, this development represented a profound betrayal of the original purpose of their organisation, as new Redmondite branches mushroomed across the country. Moderate elements in the original leadership accepted the imposition of the Irish Parliamentary Party's nominees onto the Volunteer executive, convinced that it was the only way to protect the movement from being obliterated. For the militants, however, the power grab by Redmond represented the destruction of their original vision.

Redmond's dramatic pledge in September 1914 to enlist the Volunteers in the European conflict, 'where ever the firing line extended', offered an opportunity to the original leaders to re-exert their control by splitting from the larger body and forming the much smaller Irish Volunteers, in opposition to the National Volunteers. The Irish Volunteer Convention in November 1914 broke away from Redmond and voted 'to repudiate the claim of any man to offer up the blood and lives of the sons of Irishmen and Irishwomen to the service of the British Empire'.[8] The constitution of the new Irish Volunteers committed the organisation 'to secure and maintain the rights and liberties common to all the people of Ireland', 'to train, discipline and equip for this purpose an Irish Volunteer Force' and 'to unite in the service of Ireland, Irishmen of every creed and of every party and class'.[9]

Irishmen joined the British forces for a variety of complex reasons.[10] For nationalists, the appeal to patriotism and a sense of duty espoused by nationalist leaders and recruitment propaganda had a formative influence, at least during the early months of the war. Economic necessity was a significant factor in urban areas, however, where young men were more inclined than their rural counterparts to consider joining. For the farming community, the war brought an economic boom, accounting, in part, for the reluctance of farmers' sons to enlist. For unionists, the war had a deeper psychological significance as appeals to patriotism and to the British Empire went to the core of their identity. Young Protestant men could now prove their loyalty and Britishness in the most pragmatic way.

FOLLOWING SEVEN IMAGES: Recruitment posters for the British war effort sought to portray fighting in the First World War as a patriotic duty for Irishmen. Employing emotive motifs, enlistment was portrayed as a moral imperative. NLI

"I'll go too!"

THE
REAL IRISH SPIRIT.

WHO CAN BEAT THIS PLUCKY FOUR?

BUT ALL THE SAME WE'RE WANTING MORE

JAMES WALKER (Dublin.) Ltd. DUBLIN.

W.T.P. 47.7.500 6/15

·AN ENQUIRY FROM THE FRONT·

"When are the other boys COMING?"

M°CAW, STEVENSON & ORR, LTD., DUBLIN & BELFAST—P.3173/7590   Issued by the Central Council for the Organization of Recruiting in Ireland.

Can You any longer resist the Call?

Issued by the Department of Recruiting for Ireland.

M'CAW, STEVENSON & ORR LTD. DUBLIN & BELFAST

THE CALL TO ARMS

IRISHMEN
DONT YOU HEAR IT?

DAVID ALLEN & SONS LTD
40 Gt Brunswick St
DUBLIN.
(Copyright Reg.)

W.I 1725 20000 7/16 HMSO

"YOUR FIRST DUTY
IS TO TAKE YOUR PART IN
ENDING
THE WAR."

Mr. J. E. REDMOND, M.P.
at Waterford, 23rd August, 1915.

JOIN AN
IRISH REGIMENT
· TO-DAY ·

Farmers of Ireland

JOIN UP & DEFEND

your possessions.

John Redmond (1856–1918), leader of the Irish Parliamentary Party, addressing a recruitment meeting for the British Army at the outbreak of the First World War. Respectable nationalists addressed such meetings across Ireland. NLI

Redmond's speech in September 1914 confirmed the IRB's suspicions about his intentions and provided the original Volunteer executive with justification to dissolve their enforced alliance with Redmond's supporters.[11] The hard-line group bluntly repudiated Redmond's position. They reiterated the objectives in the original manifesto, explicitly rejecting Redmond's offer of support to the British military: 'The first and main object, and the immediate purpose for which the Volunteers had been initially founded, was to secure national legislative and executive autonomy and this object had been again stated in the clearest terms on behalf of the Irish Parliamentary Party, in taking up a position of definite relations with the Irish Volunteer organisation.'[12] The new provisional committee enshrined in their constitution the principles of 'securing and maintaining the rights and liberties common to all the people

John Redmond addressing a recruitment meeting. These meetings were often boisterous affairs, with heckling and scuffles not uncommon. NLI

of Ireland, to render service to a national government when such is established and to unite in the service of Ireland Irishmen of every creed and of every party and class'. A new county battalion structure was established, administered by a board of delegates from each company, and a representative from each county was in turn elected to a general council.[13] A military staff was approved, comprising Eoin Mac Néill, Patrick Pearse, Joseph Plunkett, Thomas MacDonagh, Bulmer Hobson and Michael O'Rahilly.[14] Pearse assured the Clan na Gael leadership in America that 'we will have pulled the Volunteers straight. No matter how badly things look, no matter what accounts you hear of loyalty and recruiting, rely upon the men here to do all that is possible. If at anytime, we are quiet, it is because we are awaiting a favourable moment.'[15] Following the split, the bulk of the Volunteers, estimated in December 1914 at 156,750, supported Redmond.[16]

John Redmond *(centre)* and his brother William *(left)* represented the respectable nationalist opinion in Ireland that the Allies in Europe were fighting a just war and should be supported. NLI

John Redmond *(second from right)* inspecting the Volunteers. Redmond's support for the Volunteers in May 1914 fundamentally transformed the political character of the new movement. NLI

John Redmond *(right)* and a Catholic archbishop. The Catholic hierarchy enthusiastically supported the Irish Parliamentary Party's campaign for Home Rule and looked forward to playing a prominent role in the new state with the granting of devolution. NLI

John Redmond *(second from left)* inspecting a parade of Volunteers in the summer of 1914. NLI

John Redmond is presented with a flag by a parade of Volunteers in the summer of 1914. NLI

REDMOND IN HIS LATEST ROLE.

The Irish Political Charlie Chaplin, With Apologies to the Real Charlie.

ABOVE: Republicans mocked John Redmond's support of the British war effort and attempted to depict him as a political joke, as in this cartoon (*c.* 1915).

FACING PAGE: As the First World War progressed, republicans sought to portray Redmond as being directly responsible for the deaths of thousands of Irishmen, as in this anti-recruitment poster (*c.* 1915). NLI

Handbills such as this this were distributed by young republicans at recruitment meetings to discourage men from enlisting in the military. NLI

Any Irishman joining England's Army, Navy, or Police Force, takes his stand in the camp of the garrison, he is a traitor to his Country, and an enemy of his People. IRISHMEN, SPURN THE SAXON SHILLING.

The small but steady growth of the Irish Volunteers accelerated as the war dragged on, as fear of conscription gripped nationalist Ireland. The popular political sentiment was conveyed by the Inspector General at the end of September: 'The Irish Volunteers number 184,000 men, and are spread over the whole country from north to south; but no progress whatsoever was made during the month in organisation. It possesses about 7,000 rifles of various patterns. It is a strong force on paper, but otherwise without officers, and untrained, is little better than a huge mob.'[17] Anger at conscription nurtured a growing climate of defiance and the emboldened Irish Volunteers carried out elaborate public demonstrations. For the first time, the Catholic clergy appeared at these.

While the IRB military council had been planning for a Rising since the outbreak of the First World War, a shortage of rifles, ammunition and basic equipment limited its capacity to prepare adequately. Simon Donnelly, Captain of C Company of the 3rd Dublin Battalion, believed that 'the vast majority of men went into action during Easter Week without having fired one round of ball ammunition. The arms they possessed were mostly of an obsolete pattern.'[18] By April 1916, senior officers in the Irish Volunteers were aware that significant manoeuvres were looming, but specific details were confined to an elite few. Volunteer Éamon Bulfin recalled, 'there was never any actual specific mention of a rising. You got the feeling that this thing was in the air and by putting two and two together, but there was never any mention of any date.'[19] Volunteer Tom Byrne remembered, 'A few months before Easter, 1916, it was generally understood that there would be a fight.'[20]

Postcards such as this were designed to mock the military prowess of the British Army. NLI

IRISHMEN

the British Government wants you to

FIGHT

the battles of your Countries oppressor

AGAINST

a nation that never injured you. It says that if you do not go willingly , it will use the Militia Ballot Act to compel you to leave your home and country to slaughter

THE GERMANS

Dont go. If you must fight , fight at home, for the Independence of Ireland. Band yourselves together to resist . Select in your district spots suitable for entrenchments , objects suitable for barricades lay in stores of provisions , choose men capable of leadership , and

FIGHT FOR IRELAND IN IRELAND·

Dont trust promises from England. Arm yourselves, be ready to resist the Act and they will think twice before they put it in force .

Anti-recruitment leaflets were distributed widely, and many republicans were prosecuted for being in possession of leaflets such as this one. NLI

"Seaġan buiḋe"

BLUFF

DECEIT

HOLY BIBLE

WHISKY OPIUM

"THE SECRET OF ENGLAND'S GREATNESS"

In anti-recruitment leaflets such as this, republicans sought to depict British imperialism as immoral and established through deceit, conquest and exploitation. NLI

An Irish Volunteers postcard. The Volunteers sought to depict themselves as following in the path of previous generations of patriots. NLI

The Battle of Vinegar Hill, Co. Wexford, 21st June, 1798.
The insurgents occupied the hill, down the slopes of which they repeatedly drove their assailants, but, lacking ammunition, were themselves ultimately compelled to retire before superior numbers.

A postcard depicting the Battle of Vinegar Hill. The centenary of the 1798 Rebellion had been celebrated by all shades of nationalists, and the Volunteers saw themselves as the inheritors of the republican tradition. NLI

RIGHT: A poster commemorating Irish participation in the Battle of Ramillies between England and France in 1706. Recruiting officers sought to appeal to the historical tradition of Irishmen fighting in European armies. NLI

BELOW: Joseph McGarrity's membership certificate of Na Fianna Éireann. McGarrity (1874–1940) was a pivotal fundraiser in Philadelphia for the Irish Volunteers. NLI

Na Fianna Éireann

Na Fianna Éireann was a republican Boy Scout movement that became associated with the Irish Volunteers in 1913. A number of members and former members played important roles in the Rebellion. Founded in 1909 by Bulmer Hobson, Pádraig Ó Riain, Countess Markievicz and other militant nationalists, the organisation was part of a wider European trend that saw the emergence of pseudo-military youth movements at the beginning of the twentieth century.[21] The organisation was conceived as an alternative to Robert Baden-Powell's Anglocentric Boy Scout movement, founded in 1908, and the Anglican Boys' Brigade, founded in Glasgow in 1883. Bulmer Hobson originally formed a unit of Na Fianna in Belfast in 1902.[22] The group was re-established in Dublin in 1909 with the intention of counteracting the British Scout movements, keeping young boys off the streets and out of trouble, and developing a resource for militant nationalism.[23]

Hobson originally suggested the idea to Countess Markievicz and Helena Molony. Markievicz agreed to rent a hall on Dublin's Camden Street, and advertisements were placed in the Gaelic League newspaper, *An Claidheamh Soluis*. There was resentment of Markievicz on account of her privileged social status, and despite her financial support of the group. Hobson recalled: 'I had on many occasions to point out privately that they [Na Fianna members] could not accept her financial help and refuse her membership or office. This feeling against the presence of a woman in the organisation continued in varying degrees of intensity for many years and probably never completely disappeared.'[24]

Committed members, including Seán Heuston, Seán McLoughlin, Garry Holohan (Gearóid Ó hUallacháin) and Leo Henderson, displayed courage and leadership during the Rebellion that belied their youth. Seán Heuston, executed for his defence of the Mendicity Institute, was vice-commandant of the Dublin brigade of Na Fianna. Con Colbert, executed for his role at Marrowbone Lane, had previously been a senior member, and Liam Mellows, who led the Galway Volunteers, had formerly been a Na Fianna organiser. Na Fianna members were responsible for the attack on the Magazine Fort in the Phoenix Park that was to have signalled the start of the Rising. The attack was a limited success when the group failed to gain access to the weapons and explosives stored in the depot. Members of this unit proceeded to join garrisons across the city, with several fighting in the Church Street area and the GPO.

Irish Volunteers on parade with arms they had landed at Howth in north County Dublin on 26 July 1914. NLI

The landing of arms was a major propaganda boost for the Irish Volunteers, pictured here on the day they landed, 26 July 1914. Later that evening, the King's Own Scottish Borderers killed four civilians in Dublin city centre. NLI

Enthusiastic supporters applaud as the arms landed at Howth are taken away, 26 July 1914. NLI

The funeral of Fenian leader Jeremiah O'Donovan Rossa (1831–1915) in August 1915 provided the Volunteers with an opportunity to display their capacity to organise a large public spectacle through the streets of the capital. Here, Patrick Pearse can be seen at the graveside.

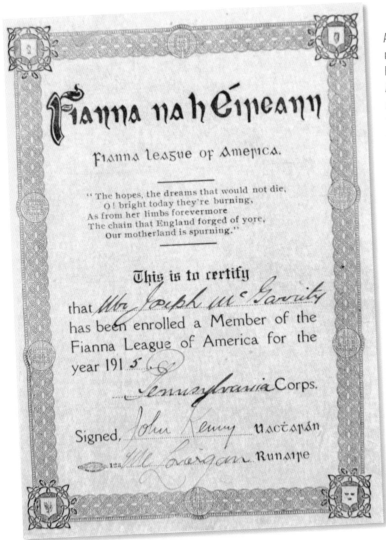

A certificate of membership of the Fianna League of America. Many Irish Americans retained their connections to their homeland, and anti-British sentiment facilitated the raising of vital funds for the Volunteers in cities such as Chicago, Boston and New York.
NLI

Cumann na mBan

Far from being passive, many Irishwomen were active in the various movements that promoted separatism in the first two decades of the nineteenth century. Cumann na mBan, a separate organisation from the Irish Volunteers, served as a women's auxiliary, with members acting as couriers, nurses and cooks during the 1916 Rising.[25] Most women were unarmed but their participation in the Rising demanded immense commitment. Unlike the Volunteers, the Irish Citizen Army (ICA) actively

IRISH VOLUNTEERS.

THE WOMEN'S SECTION OF THE VOLUNTEER MOVEMENT.

Cumann na mBan
(THE IRISHWOMEN'S COUNCIL),

Headquarters :—206 Great Brunswick St.

IRISHWOMEN, JOIN THE
VOLUNTEER MOVEMENT
AND BECOME MEMBERS OF THE ABOVE ORGANISATION.

First Aid and Ambulance Classes. Reserve Corps of Trained Nurses. Drill, and Rifle Practice.

Contribute to our Equipment Fund, which has already bought Rifles for the Volunteers.

Intending Members, join the nearest Branch, or communicate with the Hon. Secretary, Cumann na mBan, 206 Great Brunswick Street, Dublin.

BRANCHES IN EVERY COUNTY IN IRELAND.

Devereux, Newth and Co., Printers, Dublin.

Cumann na mBan recruitment poster. Members studied first aid and participated in a range of fundraising and propaganda activities in advance of the Rising, in which the organisation played a crucial role. NLI promoted female officers. Countess Markievicz was second-in-command to Michael Mallin at St Stephen's Green during the Rising, while Dr Kathleen Lynn fought as an officer at City Hall. Lynn and Markievicz were exceptional characters, widely admired by other women. The active women in the separatist organisations were mainly young and unmarried, and consequently their male colleagues frequently referred to them as 'the girls'.

Cumann na mBan was founded in Wynn's Hotel in Dublin in April 1914. One hundred women attended the inaugural meeting, presided over by Agnes O'Farrelly. The movement was conceived as a support group for the Volunteers – 'a non-partisan non-sectional national organisation for women' of 'Irish birth or descent alone'. The group's early headquarters was at 8 D'Olier Street, and it claimed to have sixty-three branches across the country by October 1914.[26] Along with first-aid and ambulance classes, the organisation engaged 'in any vital national work in which its activities [were] needed'. These activities included raising money for the 'Defence of Ireland Fund', for rifles and other military supplies. The Cumann na mBan leadership rejected the limitations of contemporary gender roles, and through its endeavours repudiated the notion that, as Helena Molony phrased it, 'the sphere of women is bounded by frying pans and fashion plates'.[27]

The initial movement was organised by older, middle-class women, several of whom – including Louise Gavan Duffy, Agnes Mac Néill and Jennie Wyse-Power – were from privileged backgrounds. Other early members included Elizabeth Bloxham, a Protestant schoolteacher from Castlebar, County Mayo, and Mary Colum, a literary critic and editor.[28] Leading activist and Abbey Theatre actor Máire Nic Shiubhlaigh recalled, 'at the beginning, before belief in the wisdom of insurrection rather than debate became widespread, it was not the military organisation it became'.[29] Its initial 'respectable' character was reflected in the membership of its first provisional committee. The 'suggested activities' for branches were set out as 'First aid, home nursing, drill and signalling and rifle practice'.[30]

The split in the Volunteer movement in October 1914 (following John Redmond's pledge to support the British War effort) was replicated in Cumann na mBan and generated bitterness between former comrades. While the leadership sided against Redmond and gave its allegiance to the Irish Volunteers, Cumann na mBan lost most of its members. A Cumann

Central Branch

Cumann na mBan

MEETS

Every Tuesday and Friday, at 8 p.m.

AT

25 Parnell Square

PROGRAMME OF WORK.

TUESDAY—FIRST-AID LECTURES AND PRACTICAL DEMONSTRATIONS.

FRIDAY—MILITARY TRAINING, including PHYSICAL DRILL, SQUAD DRILL, MORSE AND SEMAPHORE SIGNALLING.

Irish women willing to assist in Cumann na mBan work for **OUR OWN COUNTRY** can enrol any meeting night.

YEARLY SUBSCRIPTION ... ... 2s. 6d.

Any communications by letter should be addressed

SECRETARY,

CENTRAL BRANCH,

CUMANN NA mBAN,

25 PARNELL SQUARE, DUBLIN.

7

ABOVE AND FACING PAGE: Cumann na mBan members were encouraged to take first-aid lessons, undertake military training and fundraise for the arming of the Irish Volunteers, as can be seen in this recruitment leaflet and the organisation's constitution. NLI

Cumann na mban
(Irish Women's Council.)

OBJECTS.

1. To advance the cause of Irish liberty.

2. To organise Irishwomen in furtherance of this object.

3. To assist in arming and equipping a body of Irishmen for the defence of Ireland.

4. To form a Fund for these purposes, to be called " The Defence of Ireland Fund."

CONSTITUTION.

1. For the time being, the direction of the Branches will be carried on by the Provisional Committee.

2. Branches will be formed throughout the country, pledged to the Constitution, and directed in a general way by the Provisional Committee.

3. Members will be expected, in addition to their local subscriptions, to support the " Defence of Ireland Fund " by subscription or otherwise.

na mBan pamphlet from 1915 claimed, 'We had come as it were to the borders of the promised land – so near that we could see its beauties and its wealth; and suddenly we were turned back, and told we must wander again for an indefinite period in the wilderness.'[31] Following re-organisation, a younger, more working-class and less 'respectable' group came to the forefront, and included Winifred Carney and Helena Molony.

THE ★IRISH★ VOLUNTEER ★

⚜ ⚜ An c-óglác ⚜ ⚜ .★★★

Vol. 1. No 43   **Saturday, November 28, 1914**   *Price, 1d.*

From the ⚜ Outpost

No "Double Duty."

The disorganisation that was noticeable in many districts after the proclamation of a double duty for Irish Volunteers has now almost passed away. The men who came into the ranks at the behest of political leaders have realised that their proper places are in the clubs and leagues and that an armed organisation is not in consonance with their ideals of service of Ireland. If they have not got over the moral turpitude of carrying a rifle to defend Irish liberties they have at least lived down the disgrace that the politicians told us would forever attach to the "stay-at-home Volunteers," and are now in the main stay-at-home non-Volunteers. There is scarcely a dozen real armed corps in Ireland believing, or professing to believe, in the double duty joke, but there are hundreds of corps drilled, armed and disciplined who believe that their first duty is to Ireland and who mean to perform that duty.

Getting Ready.

No slacking off in Volunteer work is apparent anywhere. Rifle practice and field work claim the best energies of the men everywhere, and gratifying progress has been made in every county in Ireland. The issue is as clear as ever, the need of training and arms more apparent than ever, and the means to achieve the end for which the Volunteers were started more apparent also. Never did circumstances so combine to hearten Irishmen in the work of preparation, and never has Ireland so well responded to the nation's call. North and South, East and West the army of Ireland is at work, and in every village in Ireland there is the means of comparison between the Irish Volunteer and the English soldier, and the comparison is far and away in favour of the former. Man for man the Volunteers are the superior in physique, in discipline, in intelligence and initiative, and better still, in having a clear conception of duty and patriotism in which neither money nor self-gratification counts. It is no wonder that envious eyes are cast upon the marching ranks of stalwart Irishmen and that so many attempts are made to win their services for abroad, for to-day in Ireland there is an army worthy of the best traditions of the best soldier nation in Europe.

Arms.

Leaving aside the gas pipe rifles there is in Ireland a good number of service rifles, which in the hands of skilled men would do excellent work. The idea hitherto held that everything depended upon the rifle is giving place to an argument equally fallacious, that everything depends upon the man. The highest authorities on rifle-shooting are now agreed that given practically any pattern of recent rifle, with men trained to use it, the results will be far better than the latest magazine rifle in the hands of unskilled men. Part of the armies engaged in the present war are armed with what in this country is generally known as the "Howth rifle," and their shooting is regarded as reaching a high standard of efficiency in comparison with troops armed with the latest Service rifle. Of course it should be the aim of every Volunteer to acquire the latest and best magazine rifle, but, failing that, he should have no hesitation in getting a single-shot Howth or Martini Enfield. But there is no use in getting either unless pains are taken to become familiar with the weapon, to practice with it and to acquire such a degree of efficiency with it as will inspire confidence in it and in himself.

Rifle Ranges.

How is this confidence to be acquired? Simply by practice. And there are ample facilities for rifle practice in Ireland In the country particularly every glen is a rifle range and every hill a means of fixing a target or of utilising as targets features already existing. The Volunteer should aim at making the rifle just as much a necessity of his ordinary avocations as a watch or a bicycle, and should make a greater effort to be a good shot than a good cyclist or a good hurler or athlete. Above all, the man who is fortunate enough to live in the country has exceptional advantages for becoming proficient in field work and for judging distances, without which the rifle is of comparatively little value.

Country Craft.

As well as the patriotism that is founded upon the love of the people and the institutions and separate individuality of the national temperament, there is a love of the physical aspect of the country itself. There is as much individuality in a field as in a man to the nature lover, and an Irish quartz rock is as different from an English quartz as an Irishman is different from an Englishman, and the traveller who has seen many lands feels the difference between the topography of various countries at a moment's notice. There is, of course, a corresponding difference between the towns of different nations, but it is not so pronounced, for the artificial life of the town that gave rise to the town itself at first and continues there afterwards has taken on a cosmopolitanism from un-national or outside associations that weakens its distinctive characteristics. The Volunteers should get away from the towns, away from the parade grounds and the ceremonial of the streets out to the stimulating influence of the country itself. Among the rocks and the marshes and the hedges the man feels the confidence of self; in the town he is only a unit swayed by the selfishness and commercialism of which every town is largely composed. In the country the issue is always clear, and patriotism is lived and felt, not an emotion that one can argue oneself into by logic. Above all, take a rifle, even though you don't get an opportunity to use it; it will help you to fit in with a different scheme of things, and unconsciously you will adapt yourself to the other conditions in which the rifle will be of supreme importance. An ordinary Irish landscape is an open book from which an intelligent Irishman can learn more about war in one hour than in a week spent on books written by the greatest masters of military strategy.

Miniature Rifles

For the winter the miniature rifle will be to a great extent the weapon for practice and amusement. Any ordinary hall is easily converted into a miniature range and no extra fittings are required except a bullet-catcher, which can easily be improvised and targets. While there is some diversity of opinion as to the ultimate utility of the miniature, there is no doubt that the Volunteer who can use any rifle well will be easily trained to use every rifle well, and the training in using the sights, in training the eye and controlling the muscles, and in acquiring a mastery over the weapon is a great asset in taking up practice with the service rifle. For amusement during the long nights, too, there is nothing in the world to compare with the rifle. Billiards are poor and flat compared to the range, and ever so many can compete at the one time. Not a town in Ireland but has a hall capable of being fitted up in a few hours as a first-class miniature range. Let us make a start, and when the spring comes we will have thousands of good miniature shots (excellent for street work), and potential shots with the service rifle.

The Irish Volunteer newspaper promoted the aims of the organisation, with articles on

German travel papers of Joseph Mary Plunkett (1887–1916). Plunkett travelled to Germany in March 1915 in an effort to attain support for an armed Rising in Ireland. NLI

Inġiniḋe na hÉireann.

IRISH GIRLS!

Ireland has need of the loving service of all her children. Irishwomen do not sufficiently realize the power they have to help or hinder the cause of Ireland's freedom.

If they did we should not see the sad sight of Irish girls walking through the streets with men wearing the uniform of Ireland's oppressor.

No man can serve two masters; no man can honestly serve Ireland and serve England. The Irishman who has chosen to wear the English uniform has chosen to serve the enemy of Ireland, and it is the duty of every Irishwoman, who believes in the freedom of Ireland, to show her disapproval of his conduct by shunning his company.

Irish girls who walk with Irishmen wearing England's uniform, remember you are walking with traitors. Irish girls who walk with English soldiers, remember you are walking with your country's enemies, and with men who are unfit to be the companions of any girl, for it is well known that the English army is the most degraded and immoral army in Europe, chiefly recruited in the slums of English cities, among men of the lowest and most depraved characters. You endanger your purity and honour by associating with such men, and you insult your Motherland. Hearken to the words of Father Kavanagh, the Irish Franciscan Patriot Priest, who pronounces it a heinous crime against Ireland, for Irishmen to join the forces of robber England. Do you think it is less a crime for Irish girls to honour these men with their company. Remember the history of your country. Remember the women of Limerick and the glorious patriot women of the great rebellion of '98, and let us, who are their descendants try to be worthy of them. What would those noble women think if they knew their daughters were associating with men belonging to that army, which has so often wrought ruin and havoc in Ireland, and murdered in cold blood thousands of Irishwomen and children. What English soldiers have done in Ireland in the past they would do again if ordered to do so. They would slaughter our kith and kin and murder women and children again as unhesitatingly as they hemmed in the helpless Boer women and children in those horrible concentration camps, where ten thousand little Boer children died from want and suffering.

Irish girls make a vow, not only that you will yourselves refuse to associate with any man who wears an English uniform, but that you will also try and induce your girl companions to do the same.

Women's influence is strong. Let us see, fellow-countrywomen, that we use it to the fullest for the Glory of God, and for the honour and Freedom of Ireland.

Inġiniḋe na hÉireann.

Inġiniḋe na hÉireann are very anxious to get the co-operation of any girl who reads this handbill and feels she would like to help in working for Ireland's freedom and trying to save innocent country girls from the great danger which their thoughtless association with soldiers exposes them to. The Secretaries are always to be seen on Thursday evenings between 8 and 10 o'clock at Dún Inġiniḋe, 22 North Great George's Street, Dublin, and we appeal to all Irishwomen to help us in this great social and national work.

FACING PAGE: Handbill distributed by Inghinidhe na hÉireann ('Daughters of Ireland') discouraging girls from associating with British soldiers. The organisation was formed by Maud Gonne, Helena Molony and others at the turn of the century to provide 'wholesome' Gaelic and patriotic activities for Irish girls. NLI

BELOW: Links between the Irish in America and revolutionaries at home were fundamental during the struggle for independence. Postcards such as this were popular throughout the period. NLI

The Irish Citizen Army

The involvement of almost 250 Irish Citizen Army members in the 1916 Rebellion assured the movement's place in Irish nationalist history.[32] In its initial phase, the Citizen Army lacked a coherent role, structure or purpose and its formation was largely symbolic. As the 1913 Lockout entered its third month, the idea of a workers' protection force offered a stimulus for the increasingly desperate strikers. It was left to a most unlikely figure to organise and train the new force: Captain James R. White, DSO, of the Gordon Highlanders, only son of Field Marshal Sir George White, hero of the Siege of Ladysmith during the Boer War. White, a Protestant supporter of the Home Rule movement, came to Dublin from Broughshane, County Antrim, at the outbreak of the dispute.[33] James Connolly subsequently endorsed White's proposal and told the locked-out workers that the

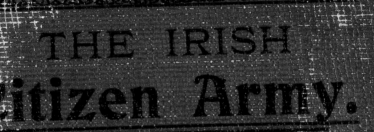

THE IRISH
Citizen Army.

MEMBER'S CARD,
1914.

Chairman of Council :
JIM LARKIN.
Hon. Secretary :
SEAGHAN O'CATHASAIGH.
Hon. Treasurers :
COUNTESS MARKIEVICZ,
RICHARD BRADFORD.

Go Scuipip Dia an Rac Opaipi.

A membership card for the Irish Citizen Army, with writer Sean O'Casey ('Seaghan O'Cathasaigh') listed as Honorary Secretary. O'Casey later left the organisation in protest at

enrolment of a Citizen Army 'was another feature of their programme'. 'A time was coming when that blow would have to be struck, for engaged in a revolutionary movement as they were', Connolly wrote, 'they would pull down civilisation itself and go down with it rather than surrender or be beaten.'[34]

The prospects for a popular workers' militia were initially positive. Locked-out men turned out for weekend parades from Liberty Hall to Croydon Park. In early December, thousands of men marched from Liberty Hall and were told by Larkin to 'wait for a short time and you will be fully armed and we'll see then who will resist us'.[35] Irish Citizen Army members wearing ICA armbands appeared at pickets and meetings across the city, armed with hurleys and sticks. Sean O'Casey concluded that the major obstacles hindering the progress of the movement were 'the frequent arrests of the Labour leaders; the gradual and humiliating weakening of the workers' resistance to the pressure of the employers; the malignant penalising of the Irish Transport Union by the hierarchy of commerce; and the establishment in the Rotunda Rink on 25 October 1914 [sic] of the Irish National Volunteers'.[36]

After the defeat of the workers in January 1914, the Citizen Army lacked a clear role in the labour movement. Jack White and Sean O'Casey revived the organisation in March 1914 and for the first time a formal constitution and a ruling council were approved.[37] An army council was elected, with White as chairman, Jim Larkin, P. T. Daly, William Partridge, Thomas Foran and Francis Sheehy-Skeffington as vice-chairmen, and the enigmatic Richard Brannigan and Countess Markievicz as treasurers.[38]

The ITGWU underwent a fundamental change of leadership when Jim Larkin left for the United States in November 1914. He was replaced as head of the union by James Connolly and Thomas Foran. Michael Mallin, a native Dubliner and a weaver by trade, was a former British soldier who had served in India and developed a strong anti-imperial perspective. He opened a shop in the Liberties, but he lost his business due to the Lockout. He subsequently became an inspirational organiser for the ITGWU.[39]

With no pickets or meetings to protect, the new incarnation of the Citizen Army became the vehicle for Connolly's emerging philosophy of revolution. Connolly's new political stance signified a movement away from doctrinal socialism to a realignment of class and national politics into a

Handbills such as this were distributed at Trade Union meetings and workplaces across Dublin. NLI

REASONS WHY

YOU SHOULD JOIN

The Irish Citizen Army.

BECAUSE It pledges its members to work for, organise for, drill for and fight for **an Independent Ireland.**

BECAUSE It places its reliance upon the only class that never betrayed Ireland—the Irish Working Class.

BECAUSE Having a definite aim to work for there is no fear of it being paralysed in the moment of action by divisions in its Executive Body.

BECAUSE It teaches that "the sole right of owner-ship of Ireland is vested in the people of Ireland, and that that full right of ownership may, and ought to be, enforced by any and all means that God hath put within the power of man."

BECAUSE It works in harmony with the Labour and true National Movements and thus embraces all that makes for Social Welfare and National Dignity.

Companies Wanted in Every District.

RECRUITS WANTED EVERY HOUR.

Apply for further information, Secretary, Citizen Army, Liberty Hall, Dublin.

Irish Paper.]　　　*City Printing Works, 13 Stafford Street, Dublin.*

The Irish Citizen Army parading in front of Liberty Hall following the outbreak of the First World War. Situated on the Dublin quays at Beresford Place, Liberty Hall was the epicentre of the 1913 Lockout.

Liberty Hall in its Heyday
The Headquarters of James Larkin's Irish Transport Workers' Union, showing the "Citizens' Army" paraded. This Army was drilled by Captain James R. White, D.S.O., son of the late Field Marshal Sir G. White, defender of Ladysmith.
[Photo, Keogh Bros.

AN IRISH WORKERS' ARMY.

The need has arisen for the embodiment of a disciplined force of the workers of Ireland,

(1) To defend the country against foreign aggression;

(2) To defend the workers against attack during labour disputes;

(3) To assert and maintain the rights of the workers as citizens; and

(4) To support the movement towards the establishment of a Workers' Republic.

It has been decided that steps shall be taken at once to enrol such a force throughout Ireland. For this purpose a temporary Committee has been formed consisting of five representatives of the Irish Citizen Army, and five representatives of the Trade Union movement.

Every member of the proposed Workers' Army shall be, wherever possible, a member of a Trade Union recognised by the Irish Labour Party and Trade Union Congress. A beginning is to be made by the enrolment in each local area of a nucleus of reliable men, preferably those who are already trained.

When a sufficient number of local units has been formed a representative Convention will be called together in Dublin to put the organisation on a permanent basis.

I, the undersigned, am willing to join an Irish Workers' Army on the basis outlined above:—

Name..

Address.....................................

....

Occupation.................................

Date..

WEST. PRINTER, CAPEL ST,

An early application form for the Irish Citizen Army. NLI

The Dublin Citizen Army.

By Dún Laeṁi.

(Air—The Rakes of Mallow)

A SONG FOR THE IRISH TRANSPORT AND GENERAL WORKERS' UNION.

Come, my boys, and sing the glory
Of our comrades famed in story,
Who when Dublin's streets were gory,
   Fought in the Citizen Army!
Dublin's Sons were Ireland's pride,
Patriots' trust in them must bide,
Heroes all, in Battle tried,
   The Irish Citizen Army.

Not for claims unjust contending,
But Pope Leo's laws defending,
Slums and vice and squalor ending,
   Strove our Citizen Army;
Slandered were those Christian men,
E'en the good deceived were then,
Till the famous Easter when
   Rose the Citizen Army!

England's Rule our Land had blighted,
Till, too long our groanings slighted,
Connolly with Sinn Fein united
   The valiant Citizen Army.
Ireland's soldiers know no fears,—
Honour them through all the years,—
Join with the Irish Volunteers,—
   The Dublin Citizen Army!

Following the Rebellion of Easter Week, the Citizen Army imploded. However, members continued to celebrate their role in the Rising, as in this song. NLI

Members of the Irish Citizen Army and the Volunteers, clergy, and mourners look on as the body of O'Donovan Rossa is lowered into his grave. NLI

single philosophy espousing a socialist republican state: 'An armed organisation of the Irish working class is a phenomenon in Ireland. Hitherto the workers of Ireland have fought as parts of the armies led by their masters, never as members of an army officered, trained, and inspired by men of their own class. Now, with arms in their hands, they propose to steer their own course, to carve their own future.'[40]

Connolly sought to build closer ties with the Irish Volunteers, who had previously felt the lash of Larkin's invective. With Larkin away in America, the ICA was steadily aligned with the Irish Volunteers, and Connolly was free to build fraternal relations with the IRB. The result was greater comradeship between the ICA and the Volunteers, which in turn nurtured the commitment and capability of Connolly's small band of followers. Older members now drifted away, to be replaced by younger, more determined fighters, committed to Connolly's philosophy of insurgency. The most immediate differences in the organisation were the imposition of formal command structures, a demand for an increased degree of personal commitment, and a new focus on the use of arms.

Connolly's blend of nationalism and socialism was a product of his commitment to making the workers' movement relevant to ordinary people. In *The Irish Worker*, Connolly advocated that the Citizen Army commit itself to meaningful action rather than the endless sterile theorising and factionalism that hitherto had characterised micro-socialist groups in Ireland. For Connolly, profound urgency was generated by the outbreak of war in July 1914, which he saw as an opportunity to strike at the heart of the British Empire. Connolly's charisma and steadiness impressed the Volunteer leadership, and the two groups put their new-found amity on show during the carefully orchestrated ceremonies surrounding the funeral of the veteran Fenian O'Donovan Rossa in August 1915. Connolly used his article 'Why the Citizen Army Honours O'Donovan Rossa' in the official programme to explain the new realities facing Irish revolutionaries: 'We are neither rash nor cowardly. We know our opportunity when we see it, and we know when it has gone.'[41]

3

EASTER WEEK:
THE FIGHT FOR DUBLIN

Hearts with one purpose alone
Through summer and winter seem
Enchanted to a stone
To trouble the living stream.
The horse that comes from the road,
The rider, the birds that range
From cloud to tumbling cloud,
Minute by minute they change;
A shadow of cloud on the stream
Changes minute by minute;
A horse-hoof slides on the brim,
And a horse plashes within it;
The long-legged moor-hens dive,
And hens to moor-cocks call,
Minute by minute they live:
The stone's in the midst of all.

'Easter, 1916' | W. B. Yeats | 25 September 1916

DURING THE EASTER RISING individual battalions faced distinct challenges and unique circumstances, and contact between the various garrisons was limited. Little is known about the secret military council's plans for the fighting. However, their tactics involved a focus on defensive rather than offensive warfare.[1] By occupying key buildings and waiting for the Crown forces to attack, the rebels handed the military initiative to their enemy, who could await reinforcements rather than attacking fortified garrisons in which their opponents initially maintained an advantage.

The preoccupation of the rebels with the defence of their garrisons and the Crown forces' reluctance to launch frontal attacks explains the eerie lack of fighting at the Jacob's Factory garrison and the outposts of the South Dublin Union garrison in Marrowbone Lane, Mount Brown and Ardee Street. Likewise, although the Volunteer leaders in the General Post Office (GPO) faced sniper fire and heavy bombardment, no concerted attempt was made to storm the building. However, the rebel outposts on Sackville Street – at Hopkins & Hopkins, Kelly's, the Imperial Hotel, the Metropole Hotel and North Earl Street – faced continuous shelling, sniper fire and heavy guns, while acting as buffers for the larger garrison at the GPO.

The primary consideration in analysing the rebels' strategy is their overwhelming lack of manpower, accentuated by their meagre resources. The countermanding order in the *Sunday Independent* by Eoin Mac Néill caused consternation among the military council and ordinary Volunteers. Simon Donnelly, Captain of C Company of the 3rd Dublin Battalion at Boland's Mill, calculated that his battalion 'went into action on Easter Monday with a maximum strength of 110 to 120 men, as against the 400 who would have paraded on Easter Sunday'.[2] Frank Robbins of the Citizen Army claimed that the failure of so many men to muster after the initial confusion on Easter Monday scuppered the leadership's plans: 'The real problem which Commandant Mallin had to contend with was the scarcity of men to occupy all the positions set out in the plans.'[3] Like many of her comrades, Helena Molony of the Citizen Army was adamant that Mac Néill's countermand would not stymie the determination to strike, come what may:

What happened on Easter Sunday overshadowed everything else. At last we had definite knowledge. If there was talk, I either did not hear

Almost 250 members of the Irish Citizen Army fought alongside the Irish Volunteers during Easter Week. They were garrisoned in the GPO, City Hall and the Royal College of Surgeons. This staged photograph shows members in their trademark slouch hats.

it or pay attention to it. My mind was preoccupied with the one thought, 'I can't believe this will really happen. I know we can depend on the Citizen Army, but what about the rest?' I saw Eoin MacNeill's countermanding order in the paper and heard the discussion in Liberty Hall. Connolly was there. They were all heartbroken, and when they were not crying they were cursing. I kept thinking, 'Does this mean that we are not going out?' There were thousands like us. It was foolish of MacNeill and those to think they could call it off. They could not. Many of us thought we would go out single-handed, if necessary.[4]

The failure of the Volunteers to occupy Dublin Castle, Trinity College and Westmoreland Street can best be understood in terms of lack of manpower. In the planning of the Rising, Florence O'Donoghue noted: 'Dominating the whole project there was an objective of greater gravity and significance than the military planning.' O'Donoghue emphasised the centrality of military action as an end in itself, as opposed to realistic tactics that reflected aspirations for victory. A preoccupation with defence was explicit in the choice of garrisons and the tactics: O'Donoghue noted that 'down to the end, the keynote is resistance'. The primacy of defensive action reflected a pragmatic assessment of available resources, but, as O'Donoghue argued, 'also has a deeper spiritual significance'. O'Donoghue concluded that the Rising was intended to be no mere blood sacrifice, but to stage a defiant protest in arms 'on a scale and duration which would ensure that it could not be dismissed' and where the military would be obliged to attack rebel garrisons with overwhelming force. Thus, no matter how the Rising ended, O'Donoghue concluded that 'it redefined in modern terms the unchanging aspiration of Irish people for sovereign control over their destinies'.[5]

Command Structure of the Dublin Brigade, Irish Volunteers, Easter 1916

	BATTALION AREA	COMMANDERS	GARRISONS
1st	North of the Liffey, west of Sackville Street	Edward Daly	Church Street, Four Courts, Mendicity Institute
2nd	North of the Liffey, east of Sackville Street	Éamon de Valera	Boland's Mill, Mount Street
3rd	South of the Liffey	Thomas MacDonagh	Jacob's Factory, St Stephen's Green
4th	Southern suburbs	Éamon Ceannt	South Dublin Union, Marrowbone Lane
5th	North County Dublin	Thomas Ashe Richard Mulcahy	North County Dublin, including Ashbourne

The experience of ordinary Volunteers during Easter Week varied considerably depending on their brigade. Several garrisons, such as the Four Courts and City Hall, were subjected to heavy shelling, constant sniping and sporadic close-quarters combat, while others, notably Jacob's Factory, saw very little hand-to-hand combat. James Slattery, stationed in Jacob's Factory, noted that 'I enjoyed a very quiet week.'[6] Volunteer Vincent Byrne recalled that he 'had a great time eating plenty of cocoa chocolate and biscuits galore'.[7] The outpost of Boland's Mill at Mount Street, on the other hand, endured an intense assault on Wednesday afternoon, resulting in dozens of dead and wounded in close-quarters fighting. Citizen Army man Frank Robbins recalled the strain that continuous sniper fire created among the rebels:

> The strain was now taking effect on a number of our men; Sergt. Joseph Doyle gave out completely for want of proper rest. This was not to be wondered at. In my own case, after the 'cease fire' order that night, I fell fast asleep, lying face down with my rifle pointing to the Shelbourne Hotel. I had had only two hours' sleep out of a period of sixty hours' duty, and that was on the roof of the College of Surgeons on Monday night. Only the ideal which inspired us enabled all to suffer and endure so much until the human frame could no longer bear the strain.[8]

Sleep deprivation was also a significant problem at Boland's Mill garrison, as Andrew McDonnell remembered: 'I cannot remember the days of the week, or day from night for that matter. They all seemed to run into one another. Sleep we got in fits and starts, and if you managed to remove your boots once in a while you were lucky. You lay down anywhere when you were told you could sleep.'[9]

The heavy bombardment from the HMS *Helga*, positioned in front of the Custom House, and concentrated attacks by the Crown forces also affected many men's nerves. Captain Joseph O'Connor noted:

> The enemy was using every possible means for blasting us out of our positions, but no matter how they battered us and no matter how intense their firing was, immediately they appeared on the scene in person, our

Dead and wounded soldiers of the Sherwood Foresters lie strewn across the road during the Battle of Mount Street. The fight at Mount Street was the Volunteers' greatest military success during the Rebellion.
KILMAINHAM GAOL ARCHIVE

Members of the Home Defence Force, named the Georgius Rex but nicknamed 'the Gorgeous Wrecks' by Dubliners, who fought in Easter Week alongside the Sherwood Foresters and the South Staffordshire Regiment.

men jumped into activity and were only too anxious to close with them and fight it out. It was a curious effect that the artillery fire had on myself, my officers and men. Needless to say, none of us had experience of being under artillery fire, or in fact in any danger at all up to the Monday of this week, but I know myself that I enjoyed the artillery fire and took a pleasure in counting the interval between the flash and the noise of the explosion.[10]

Volunteer Seán Cody was involved in heavy house-to-house fighting across the North King Street and Church Street area, which raged from late on Wednesday until Saturday evening:

I had the misfortune to become detached from my comrades and remember meeting a lady in a side street who invited me to come up to her room which was on the top flat where she said I could get a good view of the British occupying the Broadstone. I followed the lady, and seeing British soldiers in the railway sheds and behind piles of sleepers I opened fire and used up all my ammunition. There was no replying fire until I was back on the street below again when the whole house was peppered with rifle fire.[11]

The Crown forces erected roadblocks on all major exit routes from the city.

Beer barrels being used for protection by the Crown forces during Easter Week.

Captain Nicholas Laffan commanded Volunteers in the Church Street area:

When night fell the firing became more intense from all sides. The enemy made a sudden attack from Lurgan and Coleraine Streets and from the Smithfield end. This was the worst night we had. With the glare of the fires, it was hard to detect their movements, as they could attack, retire and then come in stronger numbers. I remember standing in a corner of Moore's Factory on Friday night and the rifle and machine gun fire from the enemy was so intense that to cross the room was certain death.[12]

Crown forces question clergymen in the city centre. KILMAINHAM GAOL ARCHIVE

" Sport & General.

PASSING THE MILITARY CORDON. MOTOR-CARS, EVEN WITH PASSES, WERE STOPPED AND
SEARCHED BY THE SENTRIES.

Cars are stopped and searched by the military – adding to the anger of 'respectable' citizens in the capital.
KILMAINHAM GAOL ARCHIVE

A burnt-out tram that was used as a barricade during fighting in the north inner city.

Facsimile of the Insurgent Newspaper.   Only this single issue was published.

IRISH WAR NEWS

THE IRISH REPUBLIC.

VOL. 1. No. 1   DUBLIN, TUESDAY, APRIL 25, 1916.   ONE PENNY

"IF THE GERMANS CONQUERED ENGLAND."

In the London "New Statesman" for *April 1st*, an article is published—"If the Germans Conquered England," which has the appearance of a very clever piece of satire written by an Irishman. The writer draws a picture of England under German rule, almost every detail of which exactly fits the case of Ireland at the present day. Some of the sentences are so exquisitely appropriate that it is impossible to believe that the writer had not Ireland in his mind when he wrote them. For instance :—

"England would be constantly irritated by the lofty moral utterances of German statesmen who would assert—quite sincerely, no doubt—that England was free, freer indeed than she had ever been before. Prussian freedom, they would explain, was the only real freedom, and therefore England was free. They would point to the flourishing railways and farms and colleges. They would possibly point to the contingent of M.P's, which was permitted, in spite of its deplorable disorderliness, to sit in a permanent minority in the Reich-stag. And not only would the Englishman have to listen to a constant flow of speeches of this sort ; he would find a respectable official Press secret bought over by the Government to say the same kind of things over and over, every day of the week. He would find, too, that his children were coming home from school with new ideas of history. . . . They would ask him if it was true that until the Germans came England had been an unruly country, constantly engaged in civil war. . . . The object of every schoolbook would be to make the English child grow up in the notion that the history of his country was a thing to forget, and that the one bright spot in it was the fact that it had been conquered by cultured Germ ny."

"If there was a revolt, German statesme n would deliver grave speeches about "disloyalty," " ingratitude," "reckless agitators who would ruin their country's prosperity. . . . Prussian soldiers would be encamped in every barracks—the English conscripts having been sent out of the country to be trained in Germany, or to fight the Chinese—in order to come to the aid of German morality, should English sedition come to blows with it."

"England would be exhorted to abandon her own genius in order to imitate the genius of her conquerors, to forget her own history for a larger history, to give up her own language for a "universal" language—in other words, to destroy her household gods one by one, and put in their place

Irish War News, composed by the military council of the IRB, was distributed to the citizens of Dublin at the beginning of Easter Week. NLI

General Post Office Garrison

The Rising had a theatrical component from the outset: it was designed as much to send a political and cultural message as to achieve pragmatic military aims. The rebels set out self-consciously to make history, and they wanted the most visible stage possible on which to perform their roles. The GPO was taken by the Volunteers without difficulty at noon on Monday morning. Notwithstanding the relative ease with which the rebels occupied the city, the insurrection began in a haphazard fashion and Éamon Bulfin recalled the chaos among his comrades as they entered the GPO: 'We lost three men before we got into action at all.'[13] Following the occupation of the building by around 400 rebels, hundreds of incredulous civilians gathered at the bottom of Sackville Street to watch and then cheer as the Lancers charged down the broad thoroughfare, only to be scattered ignominiously by rifle fire from the windows of the GPO. For the remainder of the week, the defenders of the building endured heavy sniper fire, and bombardment from the gunboat *Helga* from Wednesday onwards.

The garrison occupied outposts along Sackville Street throughout the week, with two posts covering O'Connell Bridge, and several more positions including the Metropole Hotel, the Imperial Hotel and the junction of North Earl Street and Sackville Street. When fleeing their outposts at O'Connell Bridge the Volunteers 'wrapped themselves round with big mattresses and ran across the street'.[14] Volunteer Frank Burke recalled: 'One never knew when an enemy sniper might find his target. Our snipers were busy too but for most of us it was a hidden enemy encircling our position.'[15] Despite the chaos around them, the composure of the rebel leaders was recalled by most Volunteers, and Joseph Good singled out Patrick Pearse for his good-natured demeanour: 'Pearse was on the ground floor and was very approachable. Volunteers spoke to him directly.'[16]

Other than sustained sniper fire throughout the week, the garrison was spared a military assault before being forced to evacuate the building by the engulfing flames of the 'Great Fire' on Friday. The shelling by the *Helga* deepened the sense of fatalism among the Volunteers: 'One shell hit a house which we had evacuated, down at the lower part of Moore Street, and flattened it out absolutely. It went down like a house of cards.'[17]

Volunteer Joseph Good recalled:

> I was posted by Oscar Traynor on the first floor of the Metropole Hotel, later to the top floor where there were about 12 young lads. Some of these were not Fianna boys or Volunteers but were civilians who had asked to join in the fight. The young lads were rather depressed; long gazing at burning buildings caused them to moan whilst they slept. They responded quickly when I made them eat something and sing a few songs. They had forgotten to eat. After they had taken a meal they were as good as I thought veterans should be.[18]

Volunteer Peadar Bracken remembered:

> At 12 noon I sent Seamus Robinson to occupy Hopkins & Hopkins with his section which was half of our force. I occupied Kelly's gunpowder shop with the other half. After I inspected the position, we barricaded the ground floor and occupied the first storey. From there I got each house linked up by boring through the walls (with crowbars got on the south side of the Bridge from a Corporation man), zigzagging in each room to save us from an enfilade of fire if any house was occupied by the enemy. I ordered all vessels to be filled with water in each room from Kelly's to Middle Abbey Street in case water was cut off. Looting was going on during the evening, and I held up several looters from the windows, and compelled them to abandon what they were taking.[19]

Volunteer Frank Thornton, Commander, Imperial Hotel, noted:

> We had quite a number of snipers posted around the building at different vantage points, some covering the dome of the Custom House from the rere top, and others from the top side windows of the Imperial. One of these, Paddy McMahon, did Trojan work and succeeded in disposing of quite a number of snipers who had been causing a terrific amount of damage in certain parts of our building.
>
> The shellfire intensified and the number of incendiary bombs increased and, what with the disaster of the falling barrels of methylated spirits, turpentine, etc. from the Hoyte's explosion, we were now a cauldron of flames. However, acting on our specific instructions, we relentlessly held on until only six of us remained on the first floor, holding both the rere and the front, mainly the rere.[20]

Crown forces posing by their armoured car. The Volunteers were heavily outgunned and had to rely on improvised explosives, revolvers and rifles – no match for the automatic weaponry possessed by the military.

LEFT AND FACING PAGE: These improvised armoured cars were hastily manufactured in the Guinness plant and were a frequent sight on the streets of the capital as soldiers sought protection from sniper fire. KILMAINHAM GAOL ARCHIVE

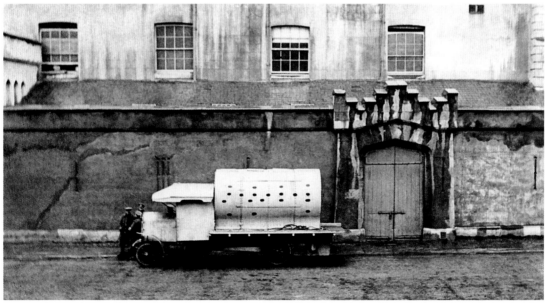

The effect of sniper fire on a Georgian window. Sniping took a heavy toll on fighters on both sides, and kept the Volunteers in a constant state of anxiety.

Irish Rebellion – May 1916. Holding a Dublin street against the Rebels.

The military take aim from behind a makeshift barrier.

A dejected Dubliner surveys the damage to the north inner city. NLI

Food shortages became a major problem for Dubliners as the week progressed. In this image
a Catholic nun feeds working-class youths in the city centre.

Heavy shelling by the Crown forces caused extensive damage in the inner city. NLI

City Hall Garrison

The occupation of City Hall by the Citizen Army was planned with the aim of impeding troops, police and administrators emerging from Dublin Castle. The small occupying force was noteworthy in that women members of the Citizen Army played a prominent role. Helena Molony and Kathleen Lynn were formidable figures in the Citizen Army, and the younger girls under their command provided first aid and other useful services. The courage and steadfastness of these women was an exceptional feature of the battle for City Hall. The attack on City Hall commenced with the shooting dead by Captain Seán Connolly of James O'Brien, an unarmed constable of the Dublin Metropolitan Police. Following the shooting, the rebels under Connolly's command were confused. Helena Molony recalled:

> The men behind Connolly did not really know they were to go through. Connolly said: 'Get in, get in' – as if they already did not know they were to go in. That guarded secrecy, not to let it look like anything other than the manoeuvres which were taking place for weeks before, may have been the reason; but certainly there was hesitation on the part of the followers. Seán Connolly shouted: 'Get in, get in'. On the flash, the gates were closed. The sentry went into his box, and began firing. I thought no one had succeeded in getting in. It breaks my heart – and all our hearts – that we did not get in.[21]

While Thomas Kain and a small detachment entered the guardroom of Dublin Castle, Connolly led his party of men and women into City Hall. Smaller detachments entered the Huguenot graveyard in Nicholas Street and the Rates Office in Synod House. These were originally regarded as strategic points in any cooperation with the Jacob's Factory garrison. On Monday evening George Norgrove brought seven Citizen Army men from the GPO to bolster the garrison. The small detachment of Citizen Army fighters held City Hall under heavy fire throughout Monday with both commanding officers, Seán Connolly and Seán O'Reilly, sustaining mortal wounds. The garrison held outposts at the junction of Parliament Street and Dame Street in the Henry & James Building and the *Dublin Evening Mail* office. A unit of Volunteers from Maynooth accompanied by a group of Hibernian Rifles occupied the Exchange Hotel on Parliament Street. The

The first casualty of Easter Week occurred at the gates of Dublin Castle, when Seán Connolly, commander of the Irish Citizen Army garrisoned in City Hall, shot dead a Dublin Metropolitan Policeman. Connolly was subsequently shot dead during the occupation of the building.

The Gates of the Upper Yard of Dublin Castle
Where the first life was lost. Here a policeman was shot, and the sentry saved the situation by closing the gates in the faces of the Insurgents. [Photo. T. W. Murphy]

group evacuated the hotel due to heavy gunfire and moved into Shortall's shop next door.[22]

The military stormed City Hall on Monday night after heavy bombardment, and the intensity of the attack overwhelmed the rebels. The attacking force was composed of soldiers of the 3rd Royal Irish Regiment, the 10th Royal Dublin Fusiliers and the 3rd Royal Irish Rifles.[23] Thus, like elsewhere in the city, Irishmen fought each other for control of the capital in the first two days of the Rebellion. Helena Molony recalled: 'At about half-past eight or nine o'clock, when nightfall came, there was a sudden bombardment. It came suddenly on us. On the roof level, on which were glass windows, and through the windows on the ground floor of the City Hall, there were machine gun bullets pouring in.'[24]

By Tuesday morning the garrison was in the hands of the military. Some rebels fled the building to evade surrendering, and William Oman of the Citizen Army was chased through the streets by an angry mob. When British troops found the group of women fighters in the shell of City Hall, they mistook them for civilian prisoners: 'The British officers thought these girls [Citizen Army members] had been taken prisoner by the rebels. They asked them: "Did they do anything to you? Were they kind to you? How many are up here?"'[25]

South Dublin Union Garrison

The 4th Battalion of the Irish Volunteers under Éamonn Ceannt occupied the sprawling South Dublin Union complex (which housed over a thousand patients and staff) on the morning of Easter Monday. The small force of sixty-two Volunteers was surrounded in close-quarters fighting by soldiers of the Royal Irish Regiment on Easter Monday and Tuesday.[26] The rebels were divided between the South Dublin Union and three outposts: Watkins' Brewery in Ardee Street, commanded by Con Colbert; Jameson's Distillery in Marrowbone Lane, commanded by Séamus Murphy; and Roe's Distillery in Mount Brown, commanded by Thomas McCarthy. These outposts played a small role in the fighting of Easter Week and were not attacked by the military, which concentrated its attacks on the South Dublin Union.

The heaviest fighting in the garrison occurred on Monday as the Volunteers carried out strategic retreats across 30 acres of buildings, outhouses, dormitories, dining halls and doctors' rooms. Combatants faced additional complications by the presence of hundreds of patients, medical staff and orderlies, who courageously remained on duty for the week. Of the seven Volunteers killed, six died on the first day of fighting and one on the second. The fighting subsided on Thursday night as the military diverted its resources elsewhere in the city, leaving the Volunteers under covering sniper fire until Sunday morning. The leadership of Éamonn Ceannt and Cathal Brugha was praised by the surviving combatants, especially their efforts to minimise civilian casualties in a fraught situation. Both sides engaged in a relatively 'clean fight', however some innocent patients and staff were killed, including Margaret Keogh (from Leighlinbridge in County Carlow), a nurse who tended the Volunteers throughout the week.

James Foran, A Company, 4th Battalion:

At about two o'clock or so on Monday, Cathal Brugha came down and said that the soldiers were getting in over the wall and he wanted a couple of men. I said, 'I'll go, because there is nothing doing here. I will get a shot up there.' I was going when some of the fellows upstairs shouted down that Ceannt sent me there and that I was not to be taken away. Two other men went up, and they were not very long up there when the two of them were shot dead. One man was Billy McDowell, and I do not know the name of the other man, he was a [house] painter.

I did not sleep for the week. I was not sleepy, and I used to walk along the corridors where I had the fellows posted here and there as sentries.[27]

Jacob's Factory Garrison

On Easter Monday morning, 114 men took possession of the sprawling Jacob's Factory, with the number increasing to 188 during the week.[28] The Jacob's Factory garrison, led by Thomas MacDonagh, was the second largest rebel post. Yet the Volunteers found themselves relatively unchallenged, with no concentrated efforts by the military to storm the garrison, and no steps taken by MacDonagh to attack the military elsewhere. The garrison initially occupied outposts in two tenement houses on Malpas Street, off Clanbrassil Street, and in buildings off Fumbally Lane and Mill Street, facing Blackpitts. Barricades were also manned in the streets to the south of the complex, New Street and Clanbrassil Street. These were

W. & R. Jacob's Factory, located on Bishop Street, was the only major employer of women in the capital. Its extensive premises was commandeered by John MacBride and Thomas MacDonagh during Easter Week.

quickly abandoned after it became clear that they served no tactical purpose. On Wednesday, twenty men under Dan Riordan sought to relieve the embattled garrison at Clanwilliam House but were turned back, with John J. O'Grady shot dead.

Despite the odd atmosphere in the garrison, Seosamh de Brún noted that 'Cheers and cries of "long live the Republic" rang throughout the building and by Wednesday the entire factory was in a state of perfect defence against a hand to hand attack from any exposed point.'[29] Pádraig O'Kelly recalled that 'the rank and file of the Volunteers in Jacob's were practically all of the middle and working-class – clerks, shop-assistants, tradesmen, labourers – "the great common people of Ireland". In Jacob's I met many GAA players whom I knew.'[30]

Seosamh de Brún, B Company, 2nd Battalion:

Incessant rifle fire was exchanged with snipers … This continued day and night, a slight lull in the dark hours before dawn, broken by occasional interchange by alert snipers, to increase in intensity at dawn when we were always 'standing too' against attack.

In the factory we found a strenuous atmosphere. Instead of the spick and span citizen soldiery as they would appear on parade, the garrison had the appearance of a laborious day's toil. Barricades were raised on windows, doorways and other points of defence, men were moving about covered with flour from head to toe, many hatless, some with coats off, actually engaged in the work of fortification, others were already in position awaiting the enemy.[31]

John MacDonagh, Lieutenant, 3rd Battalion:

MacBride's influence was useful in steadying our men. One day, an excited Volunteer, Dick Cotter, entered the headquarters room, where I was sitting with MacBride, and announced that thousands of British troops were advancing up the street. MacBride coolly replied, 'That's alright!' Thinking MacBride did not realise the importance of his message, Cotter persisted. MacBride again said, 'That's alright', and, turning to me as if continuing our conversation, said, 'So I played my king and won the game.' Dick Cotter went away, satisfied that there was nothing to be alarmed about.

We could see, towards the end of the week, the glare in the sky from the fires which were raging in O'Connell Street. This heartened us, for it showed the magnitude of the rising, which we knew would change the whole position of Ireland.[32]

St Stephen's Green and College of Surgeons Garrison

The Citizen Army under Michael Mallin and Countess Markievicz occupied St Stephen's Green with a force of 142 fighters on Easter Monday morning.[33] The rebels harried people to leave, locking the gates behind them and digging trenches and defensive fortifications. Cars were seized and overturned to block the surrounding roads and (to the incredulity of guests in the Shelbourne Hotel) a recalcitrant driver was shot dead. The garrison initially had outposts at the Harcourt Street tram station, under Richard McCormick, and two groups at Portobello Bridge and Davy's shop and pub. These outposts were meant to impede troops emerging from nearby Portobello Barracks.[34] Frank Robbins recalled: 'our job was to check and

Rebels under the command of Countess Markievicz and Michael Mallin fled to the College of Surgeons *(pictured)* on Easter Monday after their position in St Stephen's Green became untenable.

Messrs. J. & T. Davy's Shop at Portobello Bridge

"Davy's Fort," occupied by Insurgents on Easter Monday. From this point attacks were directed across the Grand Canal on the Military at Portobello Barracks.

Davy's shop and pub on Portobello Bridge in the south inner city was occupied by fighters due to its proximity to Portobello Barracks. The premises overlooked the main entry route for troops from the barracks into the city centre.

delay the advance of the British military approaching from Portobello Barracks long enough to allow the main portion of the St Stephen's Green Division to dig themselves into their allotted positions'.[35]

The decision to garrison St Stephen's Green demonstrated tactical naivety. The lack of cover in the exposed park left the insurgents vulnerable to machine gun and sniper fire from Crown forces positioned on the roof of the Shelbourne Hotel, Trinity College and the United Services Club. The lack of a sufficient number of men to garrison Trinity College or the Shelbourne Hotel, as initially planned, left the rebels vulnerable to devastating sniper fire. With several men killed by machine gun fire on Monday, the garrison evacuated St Stephen's Green on Tuesday morning and entered the College of Surgeons through York Street. The immediate object was to seek shelter from heavy gunfire, and to secure rifles and ammunition believed to be held by the officer training corps attached to the college.[36] Subject to sniper fire all week, the garrison tunnelled into surrounding buildings, including the Dublin Turkish Baths, with the intention of reaching South William Street and Grafton Street.

Frank Robbins, Irish Citizen Army, recalled:

Our Company was to get ready to break through and occupy the houses beginning from the Turkish Baths, towards South King Street. We left the College of Surgeons by the back gate. The password being given, we were admitted into the Turkish Baths building, when the operation of breaking through from house to house began. With seven-pound sledge-hammers we made a hole in each wall big enough for a man to get through on hands and knees. As the dusk fell a number of us were sent ahead along the back outhouses to gain entrance to some of the houses ahead, with instructions to work back towards the other party. By adopting this method the task was completed sooner. The reason for this move was two-fold, the first being that we should take occupation and thereby forestall a similar move if made by the opposing forces. The second was that on that very night plans were made to set Grafton Street and the northside houses of Stephen's Green on fire. Several houses on the latter side had been occupied by the British forces, one of which was the United Services Club, and had been giving a great deal of bother during the day. Hence the decision to set fire to the houses on that side of the 'Green'.

The firing of two shots was to be the signal for an intense fusillade against the Shelbourne Hotel, United Services Club, and any other positions occupied by the British military. This firing was to act as a cover for two sections of our men, under Lieuts – Kelly, I. C. A. and Kavanagh – Irish Volunteers. The former was to set fire to the houses on the corner of Stephen's Green and Grafton Street, while the latter was to accomplish the same objective, beginning at Noblett's corner. The fusillade opened promptly at 10 p.m., and was continued for some time, when an order was brought through by Countess Markievicz to cease fire.[37]

Boland's Mill Garrison

The 3rd Battalion of the Dublin Brigade of the Irish Volunteers under Éamon de Valera occupied a series of posts in and around Boland's Mill in the east of the city centre. Volunteer Joseph M. O'Byrne explained:

> [Boland's Mill] was in reality an outpost position on the left flank of the main body of the Battalion who held the line Westland Row Station – Boland's Bakery – Lansdowne Road, during Easter Week.
>
> To my Company [D Coy, 3rd Batt.] was allotted the task of holding this outpost, and of defending the main body from any attack by enemy troops who might make an advance via Ringsend Road and Brunswick Street (now Pearse Street), with a view to attacking the main body on its left flank.
>
> Besides its importance from a military stand-point, it had also the advantage of being a food centre, for the mill was well stocked with flour.[38]

The Volunteers endured sniping, heavy shelling and isolated sorties by small units of Crown forces throughout the week. Men posted along the railway line faced particular danger from sniper fire: 'Fire was rather heavy at this point and at times it was not possible to lift your head above the parapet of the trench.'[39] Seán Byrne was tasked with setting up a first-aid field station to care for the injured: 'That house was the Grand Canal Street dispensary at the corner of Clarence Street and Grand Canal Street. I was told that the occupants of the house were to be put out, and under no circumstances were they to be allowed take any documents with them.' In contravention of the accepted norms of warfare, Byrne claimed that he was fired upon from Sir Patrick Dun's Hospital (hospitals were considered exempt from combat): 'The Commandant [Éamon de Valera] made out a document to notify the public that the British were using hospitals for military purposes, and that if they continued to do so he would have no alternative but to shoot the prisoner. [The Volunteers had taken a soldier captive earlier in the week, but he was humanely treated.] That document was signed by the Commandant himself, by the prisoner, and by me. I understood that the document was to be sent to the GPO to be printed, for the purpose of having it read out in the churches.'[40] Seán O'Shea claimed that the same

Boland's Mill was a sprawling complex of buildings located close to the village of Ringsend. The garrison was commanded by Éamon de Valera during the Rebellion.

institution turned away seriously wounded Volunteers: 'John Doyle … was refused admission to Sir Patrick Dun's Hospital. He was taken home and died after considerable agony.'[41] As the week wore on, the Volunteers' palpable exhaustion was aggravated by hunger: 'our food for the week consisted of bread from the Bakery, margarine, "Oxo" cubes, tinned coffee and tea'.[42] Heavy shelling exerted a significant impact: 'Shells continued to pour into the building and it became flooded and impossible to hold.'[43]

The Volunteers achieved their greatest single military success on Easter Wednesday, when an isolated outpost of the Boland's Mill garrison, comprising seventeen Volunteers, inflicted serious casualties on the Sherwood Foresters. This engagement, which has become known as the Battle of Mount Street, was one of the few sustained direct firefights between the Volunteers and the military, and accounts for the large number of Sherwood Foresters killed during the week. Under the command of Brigadier Ernest Maconchy, the Nottingham regiments arrived in Kingstown (now Dún Laoghaire) by boat early on Wednesday morning and shortly after noon they were approaching the city. The Volunteers, under

No. 25 Northumberland Road

Seized by the Insurgents. Here a desperate affray took place, and the condition of the house shows the effects of a well-directed and continuous fire. [Photo by Chancellor.

Clanwilliam House, Clanwilliam Place

When the Sherwood Foresters approached Mount Street Canal Bridge, which faces Clanwilliam House, they were received with a terrific frontal fire from Clanwilliam House, which seriously thinned their ranks. [Photo by Chancellor.

Mount Street Bridge, with which Clanwilliam Place and Northumberland Road intersect, was the scene of Easter Week's bloodiest battle.

MOUNT STREET—1916

Reynolds

Doyle

Murphy

Malone

The insurgents who lost their lives during the Battle of Mount Street were Volunteers George Reynolds, Patrick Doyle, Richard Murphy and Michael Malone.

the command of Michael Malone, were situated in four buildings at the junction of Northumberland Road and Mount Street. The Volunteers opened fire in a frontal attack that continued until 7 p.m., with persistent attacks into the late evening. The fight ended when hand grenades were thrown into Clanwilliam House, where several fighters were billeted: the building burst into flames. Four of the seventeen fighters perished in the blaze or were shot dead.

Church Street and Four Courts Area Garrison

The most severe fighting of Easter Week took place in the north inner city. The 1st Battalion of the Dublin Volunteers occupied the Church Street and Four Courts area, which witnessed intense street fighting during the latter part of the week. The battalion was commanded by Edward Daly, with Piaras Béaslaí as vice-commandant and Eamonn Duggan as adjutant. Daly used St John's Convent on North Brunswick Street as his headquarters during the early days of Easter Week, with Fr Mathew Hall on Church Street also serving as a field hospital and headquarters. Reilly's pub at the junction of Church Street and North King Street became an outpost in the latter part of the week and was the scene of hard fighting.

The battalion had northern outposts at Church Street and North King Street, and to the south at the Four Courts, Church Street Bridge and in the Mendicity Institute on the southern quays. The most acute close-quarters

The Four Courts   *Facing River Liffey*

On Easter Monday the Courts of Justice were seized by the Insurgents. There was much brisk fighting at the Courts, which bear the evidences of machine gun fire. The Insurgents surrendered on Saturday, 29th April.   [Photo by Chancellor.

Some of the most intense fighting of Easter Week took place in the streets to the north of the Four Courts. The garrison was commanded by Edward Daly and was the scene of the North King Street massacre by the South Staffordshire Regiment on the Friday night of Easter Week.

fighting took place from Thursday onwards at the junction of Church Street and North King Street, and at the intersection of Church Street and North Brunswick Street, only a short distance away.[44] Along with the intense street fighting, sniper fire (from unseen positions) accounted for the majority of casualties.

A group of Volunteers occupied portions of the Four Courts early on Monday morning, facing no resistance. The building was reinforced, windows were smashed and snipers were posted on the roof. The large complex was considered ideal for defence, and the building served as headquarters for the battalion throughout the week. At nearby Church Street Bridge, twelve men under Peadar Clancy established an outpost with covering fire from the Records Office at the Four Courts. Additional small outposts were established along Church Street, North King Street and North Brunswick Street, as well as at the Jameson distillery on Beresford Street. These units barricaded the narrow lanes, blocking various entries into the district. Barricades were formed from whatever Volunteers could lay their hands on, including old boilers, carts, rubble and debris, along with carriages seized from a local coach maker.

From this scattered collection of outposts, sorties issued during the week into the north side of the city, to the Linenhall barracks, the North Dublin Union, the North Circular Road and Broadstone Railway Station, and to the south of the Liffey to occupy the Mendicity Institute. The occupation of houses along Church Street, North Brunswick Street and North King Street forced many residents to flee, and placed civilian homes directly in the field of battle. Snipers were positioned on rooftops and were particularly active in the northern outposts on North Brunswick Street under the command of Patrick Houlihan. He held his outpost until Sunday morning and his was the last unit to surrender.

Isolated sorties on the military commenced on Monday afternoon when a party of Lancers on horseback were fired on by the Volunteers from Chancery Place along the quayside; several were killed. Horses remained loose for the rest of the week, escalating the sense of danger and panic. A unit of Lancers remained huddled in Charles Street until Easter Thursday.[45]

On Wednesday, policemen were held prisoner by the Volunteers in the Bridewell and in the Four Courts. Prisoners were treated humanely by the Volunteers at Fr Mathew's Hall and in the Four Courts despite the ferocity of the fighting. Denis O'Callaghan led a unit to take the Linenhall barracks and burn the building down. The fire engulfed surrounding buildings and lit up the entire area on Wednesday night, spreading through neighbouring buildings until Friday.

On Thursday morning, residents began to flee the district in the face of the flames, sniper fire and obvious danger. The military, boosted by reinforcements from England, encircled the area in a tightening cordon. With their cordon in place, at daylight on Friday the military attacked the northern outposts of the garrison at North King Street, an attack that persisted until Saturday night. The South Staffordshire Regiment established its headquarters at the northern end of the garrison and fought house to house along North King Street, killing Volunteers and civilians. The Volunteers were gradually forced back to their stronger outposts to the north-west of the district, and the fighting in the North King Street and Church Street area intensified, with civilians huddled in cellars subject to increasing danger. Volunteers were now boring their way through homes, with the military advancing under the cover of armoured cars before pouring into tenement houses. Reilly's 'Fort' (the fortified pub) suffered sustained attacks on Saturday, before the Volunteers retreated towards Church Street and the net around them grew ever tighter.

Surrender

An unconditional surrender was issued by the military council after 3 o'clock on Saturday afternoon in order to save the lives of Dublin's citizens. The original surrender notice was delivered by nurse Elizabeth O'Farrell at the junction of Moore Street and Parnell Street. When General Lowe refused to accept the original surrender notice from O'Farrell, she returned to the military barricade with Patrick Pearse and the surrender was accepted. The leadership called the surrender as the flames of a great fire engulfed Sackville Street. Many Volunteers believed that the order was issued too early. While the garrisons at Jacob's Factory and the South Dublin Union could have held their positions, City Hall had collapsed, and the garrisons in the Church Street and Four Courts area, Boland's Mill and the College of Surgeons were under extreme pressure due to exhaustion.

The extensive damage to the environs of Sackville Street (renamed O'Connell Street in 1924) outraged Dubliners.

A view of Nelson's Pillar, built in 1808, from Henry Street. The pillar survived the week relatively unscathed.

The order caused heart-searching among ordinary Volunteers, many of whom wished to fight on. At the College of Surgeons, 'Commandant Mallin called a conference of the officers to discuss the advisability of moving out and taking to the hills or surrendering. The majority of them were in favour of discarding our uniforms and equipping ourselves as a flying column, but Connolly's endorsement of General Pearse's order prevented such action, as far as Commandant Mallin was concerned.'[46] Volunteer Joseph O'Byrne remembered the news arriving at Boland's Mill:

So the time wore on until noon when a message was brought to me which stunned us, and quenched in our hearts the high hopes which had never left us during that week. We were to proceed to headquarters in the Bakery with all our arms and equipment for unconditional surrender to the British, timed for one o'clock. What had happened we knew not but there was the stark reality – unconditional surrender and

Admiral Nelson surveys the ruins of the city.

the destruction for God knows how long of the movement, built up with such skill and sacrifice and in spite of tremendous opposition ... Our reunion was sad and disheartening. Our friends like ourselves were deeply depressed. Commandant de Valera, who was clearly suffering deeply under the tragedy of the occasion, came along and shook each of us by the hands.[47]

ABOVE AND FOLLOWING PAGES: The 'Great Fire of Sackville Street' devastated the north inner city. It started in Middle Abbey Street on Wednesday following heavy shelling by the Crown forces. NLI

Patrick Pearse hands the surrender notice to General Lowe at 3 o'clock on Saturday afternoon. General Lowe is accompanied by his son. The military photographer has airbrushed Nurse Elizabeth O'Farrell from Pearse's side — however, her boots are still visible.

FACING PAGE: A copy of the original surrender notice signed by Patrick Pearse, James Connolly and Thomas MacDonagh. NLI

In order to prevent the further slaughter of Dublin citizens, and in the hope of saving the lives of our followers
now surrounded and hopelessly outnumbered, the members of the
Provisional Government present at Head Quarters have agreed
to an unconditional surrender, and the Commandants of the
various districts in the City and country will order their
commands tp lay down arms.

P. H. Pearse

Dublin

29th April 1916

3.45 p.m.

I agree to these conditions for the
men only under my own command in
the Moore Street District and for the men
in Stephen's Green Command.

signed James Connolly
april 29/16

After consultation with Commandt Ceaunt I have
confirmed this order, agreeing to unconditional
surrender.

Thomas MacDonagh,
Commandant
30. IV. 1916.
3.15 p.m.

Police escort a prison van through the streets after the surrender. The relief on the constables' faces is obvious.

ABOVE AND FACING PAGE: Relieved Crown forces recuperate after the week's fighting.

Two weary insurgents pose in the ruins of their garrison.
KILMAINHAM GAOL ARCHIVE

An exhausted fighter is led through the streets by the Crown forces.

Éamon de Valera as a prisoner of the military. He commanded the Boland's Mill garrison during Easter Week. He was later to become one of the pivotal figures in Irish political history.
KILMAINHAM GAOL ARCHIVE

FOLLOWING PAGES: The Volunteers were overwhelmingly working-class and lower-middle-class men in their twenties and early thirties. This group is awaiting deportation from Richmond Barracks.

145

Republican prisoner being escorted to Kilmainham Gaol. KILMAINHAM GAOL ARCHIVE

Sinn Fein Rebellion, Dublin

Military examining Parcels before allowing Visitors to Prisoners

Prisoners' families being searched as they attempt to visit their loved ones in Richmond Barracks.
KILMAINHAM GAOL ARCHIVE

Prisoners being taken to the docks to be deported to jails across Britain. The men were subjected to verbal abuse from citizens of all social classes as they trudged through the ruins of the capital.

Major-General Sir John Maxwell *(third from left)* thanks ambulance staff for their efforts during the Rebellion. KILMAINHAM GAOL ARCHIVE

149

The ambulance services, pictured here, were overwhelmed by the scale of the casualties within the city during Easter Week. KILMAINHAM GAOL ARCHIVE

General Maxwell *(centre)* and his staff, Easter Week. KILMAINHAM GAOL ARCHIVE

Group photo featuring most of the seventy-seven Cumann na mBan members imprisoned for their participation in the Rising, taken after their release. The military was reluctant to acknowledge the role of Cumann na mBan, and deported just five women following the Rebellion.

Prime Minister Asquith *(centre)* arrived in Dublin on 12 May to see for himself the aftermath of the Rebellion.

Members of F Company, 4th Battalion of the Irish Volunteers, pose for a photograph following their release from prison. KILMAINHAM GAOL ARCHIVE

4

AFTERMATH: ALL CHANGED?

Too long a sacrifice
Can make a stone of the heart.
O when may it suffice?
That is Heaven's part, our part
To murmur name upon name,
As a mother names her child
When sleep at last has come
On limbs that had run wild.
What is it but nightfall?
No, no, not night but death;
Was it needless death after all?
For England may keep faith
For all that is done and said.

'Easter, 1916' | W. B. Yeats | 25 September 1916

PPROXIMATELY 485 civilians, 63 rebels, 128 military personnel and 3 police were killed in the fighting in Dublin city centre during Easter Week. In the immediate fallout from the Rising, the authorities breathed a sigh of relief, as the rebellion had been rapidly suppressed and it was apparently repudiated by respectable Irish opinion.[1] However, the pendulum swung rapidly again following the peremptory courts martial and executions of the leaders, and the internment of over 1,800 men (and five women). This revolution in popular opinion facilitated the obliteration of the Irish Parliamentary Party, the novel ascendancy of physical-force nationalism, the overwhelming victory of Sinn Féin in the 1918 election, and the secession of most of Ireland from the British Empire.

Martial law was declared in Dublin on Easter Tuesday, 25 April, and two further Acts quickly followed, abolishing the right to civil trial and placing the whole country under martial law.[2] Major-General William Lowe (1861–1944), who commanded the British troops in Dublin during Easter Week, was relieved of his duties on Friday afternoon by Major-General Sir

The ruins of the north inner city in the environs of Nelson's Pillar *(above)* and at the corner of Abbey Street *(facing page)*. NLI

John Maxwell (1859–1929). Maxwell, although a mothballed general, was seen as an ideal candidate for crushing the insurrection because of his experience in suppressing native unrest throughout the empire.[3] Maxwell, a bluff not-too-bright military man, was utterly ignorant of the Irish situation but was left entirely to his own devices by Asquith's government, which was focused on the war effort. He ordered an indiscriminate round-up of suspects, followed by courts martial, and he favoured harsh retribution. The result was predictable – the alienation of Irish public opinion.

As the rebel garrisons surrendered on Easter Sunday, about a thousand prisoners were marched to Richmond Barracks. Sweeps of the city swelled the mass arrests, which were extended outside Dublin on 3 May with prominent Volunteers targeted across the country. Mobile infantry columns arrested hundreds of suspects, especially in counties Wexford and Galway, where over 600 men were detained. The military eventually arrested 3,430 men and seventy-nine women. Of the men, 1,424 were quickly released after being interviewed by a military panel, while 1,836 were interned in England. All but five of the seventy-nine arrested women were released by

Corner of Abbey Street, Dublin.

The ruins of the Dublin Bread Company on Sackville Street. NLI

the end of May. Courts martial were inflicted on 170 men and one woman (Countess Markievicz – who was disappointed to avoid the death sentence). Of the 171 court-martialled, ninety were sentenced to death and eleven were acquitted. Fifteen men were executed, while the remainder had their sentences commuted.[4]

After the outbreak of the First World War in 1914, the Defence of the Realm Act (DORA) provided for trials of civilians by military courts and empowered ministers to create new offences without reference to Parliament. These military courts took two forms. The General Courts Martial (GCM), the highest form of military court, was reserved for serving officers. The Field General Courts Martial (FGCM) was quicker and easier to convene, as there was no requirement for presiding officers to be legally trained and three rather than nine officers were required.[5] DORA had been amended in Ireland in 1915 to deny civilians a civil trial in the ordinary courts, to avert the possibility of defendants being acquitted by sympathetic juries. The 1916 rebels were charged under the three-judge FGCM system. These military trials were widely regarded as suspect in Ireland.

Colonel E. W. Maconchy presided over the trials of four of those executed by firing squad, while Brigadier General Charles Blackader oversaw seven.[6] The prisoners were charged with committing an act 'prejudicial to the public safety or the defence of the realm ... for the purpose of assisting the enemy'. Connolly, Mac Diarmada and Mallin were also charged with 'attempting to cause mutiny, sedition or dissatisfaction ... among the civilian population'.[7] Courts martial were held at Richmond Barracks in Inchicore, in close proximity to Kilmainham Gaol.[8] Maxwell ordered that all trials should be conducted in secret and even the archival record was closed until 1999. These secretive proceedings elicited calls by MPs for details of the trials to be released.

None of the presiding officers had any legal training, although all were senior officers from the British battalions that had fought during Easter Week. The defendants were not permitted legal representation but were allowed to call witnesses (only a handful chose to do so). William Wylie acted as principal prosecuting council for the authorities.[9] All prisoners faced a central charge that they took part 'in an armed rebellion and in the waging of war against His Majesty, the King'.[10] Prosecution witnesses were called in each case – military officers or senior policemen who could substantiate the defendant's participation. Several appeared in numerous cases. Most trials lasted only a few minutes.[11]

All of the leaders who were subsequently executed pleaded not guilty, with the exception of William Pearse. The decision to execute some leaders and not others was arbitrary. Con Colbert, John MacBride, Michael O'Hanrahan and William Pearse were executed although they were not principal leaders, while more senior leaders – William T. Cosgrave, Éamon de Valera, Thomas Ashe and Richard Mulcahy – were reprieved as public outrage mounted as the body count rose.[12]

Civilian Casualties

Over 1,700 civilians were admitted to hospital in Dublin with injuries due to the Rebellion.[13] Civilian casualties significantly exceeded military and rebel casualties combined. The victims of Easter Week were most concentrated among the poor of Dublin city centre. The facts surrounding civilian deaths remain unclear and disputed.[14] Military enquiries were conducted only in high-profile cases and, even then, the evidence and testimony are of limited value.[15] Inquest evidence reveals the inherent bias of military courts, and their preoccupation with protecting the reputation of the Crown forces. For the vast majority of the civilian casualties, there was no legal recourse, no verified accounts of the deaths, and the victims were buried in haste.

The Irish Times published lists of people interred in Glasnevin (254), Mount Jerome (29) and Deansgrange (49) cemeteries as a direct result of the Rising.[16] These lists, collated and published in 1917, included the names, ages and addresses of the deceased.[17] Only thirty-seven of the forty-nine bodies interred in Deansgrange could be identified and twenty additional unidentified bodies were interred in Glasnevin. These figures include some combatants, but given the confusion of Easter Week, the poverty of the districts involved, and the ferocity of the fires that engulfed the north inner city, these figures may underestimate civilian deaths.

A 'Rebellion Victims' Committee' was announced by the Lord Lieutenant in October 1916 to 'inquire and report with regard to applications for payment out of public funds'. Those eligible included 'persons who had suffered loss by reason of personal injury sustained by them without misconduct or default on their part in the recent Rebellion; and dependents of deceased persons who without misconduct or default on their part, were killed or injured in the Rebellion.' The committee was chaired by Charles St. G. Orpen, the president of the Incorporated Law Society of Ireland, and included Charles H. O'Conor, inspector, Local Government Board, and J. J. Taylor, principal clerk of the Chief Secretary's office. The proceedings of the committee were conducted in private and in February 1917 details of some of 'the claims of persons whose breadwinners were killed during the suppression of the Rebellion' were published. The board received 450 applications in respect of such claims, but details regarding payments, the criteria used to assess claims, and other information surrounding the process were not disclosed.

CASUALTIES BROUGHT INTO CITY HOSPITALS DURING THE REBELLION

Hospital	Soldiers killed	Soldiers wounded	Civilians killed	Civilians wounded
Adelaide	4	2	5	17
Meath	3	5	2	57*
Coombe	1	-	-	-
Dr Steevens'	6	8	6	100*
St Vincent	-	-	4	50
Mercer	4	5	15	278*
Sir Patrick Dun	4	-	12	44
City of Dublin	19	75	9	57
Castle	6	107	16	43*
Eye and Ear	-	32	-	-
Jervis Street	3	7	40	348*
Richmond	1	-	14	200*
Mater	2	4	29	300*
King George V	11	36	-	3
Others	-	29	1	31
Morgue	1	-	37	-
Total	**70**	**310**	**191**	**1,726**

* approximate figure. Table compiled by Sergeant M. Mannion and Superintendent Owen Brien, G Division, DMP. Source: 'Reports of Police and Persons Killed or Wounded by Police, May–July 1916', WO 35/69/1, TNA, Kew.

The majority of civilian casualties came from the poverty-stricken districts of Dublin's north inner city, which were in close proximity to the fighting. Twenty-nine children are recorded as casualties. Mistaken identity, stray bullets or accidents cannot account for the large number of civilian casualties. The clusters of deaths in the North King Street, Church Street and Manor Street area, and in the districts around Marlborough Street and Moore Street, point to a more sinister motive.

Accounts of drunkenness and looting in the north inner city abound in contemporary reports and the hostility of Dublin's poorest citizens threatened the Volunteers' control of the city centre during the Rebellion; for those with loved ones fighting on the Western Front, contempt for the rebels was profound. The writer Frank O'Connor noted: 'Their sons, husbands, brothers, were at the front, fighting the Germans; the separation money flowed like water through the streets, and now the dirty pro-Germans were attacking it. Attacking the blessed separation money.'[18]

The sustained looting in the Sackville Street area and the venom directed at the insurgents were remarkable. Volunteers had orders to use all necessary force to disperse unruly crowds. Arthur Agnew, a member of the Kimmage garrison that occupied Kelly's shop overlooking O'Connell Bridge, recalled: 'Our orders were that the looters were to be stopped and made drop their loot on the street. If they failed to do this they were to be shot.'[19] Vincent Byrne, who fought at Jacob's Factory, remembered:

> When we came out on the street, a lot of soldiers' wives and, I expect, imperialistic people – men and women – came around us. They jeered and shouted at us. One man in the crowd was very aggressive. He tried to take the rifle off one of our party. Lieutenant Billy Byrne told him to keep off or he would be sorry. The man, however, made a grab at the rifle. I heard a shot ring out and saw him falling at the wall.[20]

Seosamh de Brún [Joseph Brown] recalled that local residents sought to demolish the barricades erected by the rebels off Clanbrassil Street: 'Several times they essayed to tear down the barricades, our men displayed great good temper. They seemed to know those people did not understand, at times patience became brittle and but for the knowledge that they were of the proletariat, reprisals might have followed. It was the first real lesson in actual discipline we learned.'[21] Michael Walker recalled that in the same district, 'the inhabitants of Blackpitts were very hostile, singing and dancing to English songs of a quasi-patriotic type – pelted stones at us and generally showed great opposition which eventually culminated in an attack on a Volunteer by a man who formed one of the crowd with the object of disarming the Volunteer. This man was shot and bayoneted, I believe, fatally.'[22]

The difficulty in distinguishing between civilians and rebels was retrospectively highlighted by officers of the Crown forces as justification for the deaths of civilians. Captain Archibald Dickson of the Sherwood Foresters recalled that during the fighting 'we had to sort out friends from enemies as we reached the houses'.[23] Colonel Vale of the South Staffordshire Regiment highlighted the difficulty in locating rebels in the crowded tenements: 'Locating the enemy in the congested houses was impossible, so the various buildings had to be cleared and this continued until the early morning of the 28 [May]'.[24] Lieutenant Colonel Taylor, commanding 2/6th Battalion South Staffordshire Regiment, was in charge of the occupation of houses in the North King Street area when civilians were shot dead: he claimed that 'My men were fired at and fired back, and any persons in upper rooms of houses, civilians or soldiers, might easily have been shot in that way.'[25]

There is limited validity in the argument that the military could not distinguish civilians from active fighters and, therefore, other factors need to be taken into consideration, including the poor training of conscripts fighting with the Crown forces and their consequent lack of discipline. Two regiments feature heavily in accounts of civilian deaths: the South Staffordshire Regiment and the Sherwood Foresters. The Sherwood Foresters suffered heavy casualties at Mount Street on Wednesday and the subsequent involvement of the South Staffordshire Regiment in the deaths of civilians, particularly in North King Street on Friday and Saturday of Easter Week, merits close attention. Major Ashcroft noted that, at the outbreak of the First World War, the South Staffordshire Regiment faced serious obstacles due to the 'lack of experienced officers' and 'the large number of unemployed men who looked neither fit nor disciplined, unlikely at any time to become really good soldiers of the King'.[26] Captain Gerrard of the 5th Division highlighted the ineptitude and lack of training that characterised the Sherwood Foresters: 'One of my sentries in Beggars Bush Barracks, about Tuesday evening, said to me, "I beg your pardon, Sir, I have just shot two girls." I said, "What on earth did you do that for?" He said, "I thought they were rebels. I was told they were dressed in all classes of attire"'.[27]

The Sherwood Foresters regiment was raised in Derbyshire and recruited heavily from the towns of Chesterfield, Matlock, Chapel-en-le-Frith, Staveley and Whaley Bridge.[28] At the outbreak of the First World War, the regiment consisted of eight battalions – two regular, two special service and four territorial.[29] During the war, seventeen extra battalions were raised and over 150,000 men served in the regiment, with 11,409 losing their lives. The regiment served most notably at Aisne, Somme, Ypres and Cambrai.[30]

The 2/6th Battalion of the South Staffordshire Regiment was formed in September 1914 and this Wolverhampton-based battalion was commanded by Lieutenant Colonel Taylor.[31] During the First World War, the regiment served at Mons, Suvla Bay, Egypt, the Somme, Thiepval, Messines and Ypres. In April 1916, the 59th Division was stationed in the St Albans area north of London, and their orders to go to Ireland came as a shock. Colonel Vale later commented: 'In the early morning of the 25th the 176 Staffordshire Brigade were marching to Berkhamstead anticipating a move to France. It was not until the town was reached that newspaper posters of a rebellion in Dublin indicated to the troops that Ireland was a possibility.' Even when they arrived in Dublin, many of the men believed that they were in France, and Vale claims 'one was heard to remark after hearing some civilians talking "I say, Bill, they've picked up our language pretty quick!"' Lieutenant Colonel Taylor commanded the 2/6th Battalion from April until May 1916. The 'South Staffords' arrived shortly after the Sherwood Foresters on Wednesday morning and marched straight into the bloodiest episode of the Rising at Mount Street, where the Sherwood Foresters were sustaining heavy casualties. Vale concluded that the regiment 'acquitted itself well in the most unpleasant of circumstances of the Easter Rebellion'.[32] The 59th division remained in Ireland until January 1917.[33]

The ruins of Wynn's Hotel on Abbey Street. NLI

The Destruction of Dublin City Centre

The destruction of Dublin city centre outraged Dubliners of all classes, with almost all of Sackville Street, Middle Abbey Street and the surrounding areas devastated by the fires that consumed the city centre. It is instructive to examine the nature and scale of the premises destroyed. Captain Purcell, chief of the Dublin Fire Brigade, estimated the value of buildings and stock destroyed to be £2,500,000. Fire crews had been busy extinguishing isolated fires in the vicinity of Sackville Street throughout Monday, Tuesday and Wednesday; some firefighters and bystanders were shot by sniper fire. Purcell attributed these fires to looters and noted that most of the premises had been ransacked before his men arrived.

The 'Great Fire', which engulfed the Sackville Street district, began on Thursday afternoon in Lower Abbey Street as the street was being bombarded by heavy guns. Purcell believed that the fire began in the reserve printing office of *The Irish Times* before spreading to Wynn's Hotel and then

ABOVE AND FACING PAGE: The heat from the 'Great Fire' of Sackville Street (now O'Connell Street) caused steel girders to melt and bend, with entire buildings collapsing. NLI

consuming the entire block. The Dublin Fire
Brigade was prevented from tackling the
blaze due to the cannonading of the street
and by 3 o'clock the flames had reached
Sackville Place:

> I saw the fire creeping along Abbey
> Street in both directions on both sides,
> on one hand up towards the Hibernian
> Bank at the corner of Sackville Street,
> and eastwards towards the Methodist
> Church in Lower Abbey Street, and then
> again on the south side, Wynn's Hotel
> made a terrible blaze. I saw the fire
> gradually work up to Hoyte's corner, and
> through the shops in Sackville Street
> down to the DBC [Dublin Bakery
> Company] restaurant. That being a very
> high building, I knew that it would stop
> the fire for a time, and as I saw the
> Grand Restaurant with its annex behind
> in Harbour Court at the rear, I had a
> faint hope that the DBC might survive.
> It made a brave stand for hours. Then I
> noticed an ominous light in the upper
> lantern windows. It was at once an
> indication that the place was doomed.

Little by little the smoke and flames gathered strength, and then burst
through the ventilators and windows. After another half hour, the roof
showed up alight and the lantern on top was wrapped in flames, and
the whole made a weird sight. It was then getting dark; it was about half
seven. Once that fire was fully under way, nothing could have saved the
block. It burned away all night.[34]

The fire continued to rage throughout Friday and by Saturday morning the
GPO itself was burning, forcing a rebel retreat into Moore Street. By then,
some of the most prominent buildings in the city, including the GPO and

ABOVE AND FOLLOWING PAGES : The General Post Office (GPO) was reduced to a shell in the inferno, with the roof and interior floors completely demolished. The GPO had only been reopened to the public earlier in the year after extensive renovations. NLI

the Metropole Hotel, were beyond rescue. At this point, Purcell felt that he could not order his firefighters to combat the blaze due to the continuance of rifle fire on his men and their two trucks, and he instructed his men to take cover. At 8 p.m. on Saturday night, Purcell responded to an urgent call from the staff at Jervis Street Hospital to prevent the building from being engulfed and he remained at the hospital until Sunday morning, ensuring that the evacuation of patients was not necessary.

THESE AND FOLLOWING PAGES: The inferno that engulfed Sackville Street was made worse by the many smashed windows caused by extensive looting, which created a dangerous backdraught that facilitated the spread of the fire. NLI

The wreckage of a building in the north inner city, pictured in the weeks after the Rebellion. NLI

FOLLOWING PAGES: The Dublin Fire Brigade, members of which are pictured here on the right, was unable to prevent the inferno engulfing the Sackville Street district, but did manage to save the Catholic Pro-Cathedral on Marlborough Street. NLI

177

Liberty Hall, the home
of the Irish Transport
and General Workers'
Union, as well as the
Irish Citizen Army, was
extensively damaged
during Easter Week. NLI

In the aftermath of the Rebellion, Dubliners flocked to O'Connell Bridge to see for themselves the destruction of the city. NLI

Crowds gathering to the rear of Nelson's Pillar are kept away from the crumbling ruins of Sackville Street. NLI

forces stand
on Henry Street.

THESE AND FOLLOWING PAGES: Left in ruins by the fighting and the Great Fire, the rebuilding of Sackville Street was to take several years. NLI

191

Sackville Street lies in ruins after the Rising. NLI

A conference of businessmen whose property was affected by the Rebellion was held in the Mansion House on 9 May. Chaired by William Martin Murphy, the leader of the Employers' Federation during the 1913 Lockout, the meeting saw the formation of the 'Dublin Fire and Property Losses Association'. The committee comprised some of Dublin's leading businessmen, including Charles Eason, William Bewley and Marcus Goodbody. The association's committee liaised with the authorities in respect of property owners' claims for compensation. Negotiations took place between the group and the new Under-Secretary, Sir Robert Chalmers, regarding the terms of reference for compensation, which centred around complex calculations regarding the liability of government and private insurance companies for losses sustained, and the issue of compensation for uninsured and inadequately insured property. The Goulding Committee was subsequently established to deal with compensation claims and was chaired by Sir William J. Goulding, along with representatives of several major insurance companies and independent assessors. Issues pertaining to the design and reconstruction of the city centre were set out in the 'Dublin Reconstruction Act'.

Arrests and Internments

The arrest and internment of thousands of Irishmen in the aftermath of the Rising contributed to the backlash against the administration and gave the Volunteers a significant propaganda boost. The 1,836 prisoners selected for internment were shipped to prisons in the United Kingdom, before being transferred to Frongoch internment camp in north Wales.[35] The camp, the site of an old distillery, was previously used to house German prisoners of war. Conditions at the camp were basic but in the context of the European war, adequate. Joseph Lawless, who had fought with the Fingal battalion at Ashbourne, recalled:

> The distillery buildings formed a kind of quadrangle, which were again enclosed by a ten-foot barbed wire fence with double apron entanglements on either side, the space between the buildings and the barbed wire on the north and east sides being the prisoners' exercise compound. The camp was roughly square, bounded beyond the wire by the railway on the west side, the station road running between the two camps on the north side, the east side was taken up by military quarters, including the Colonel's house, the view beyond stretching up on the wooded hillsides, while the south was bounded within fifty yards or so of the wire by a pleasant little river, which I am sure must have held a few trout.[36]

Joseph Good recalled that the treatment of the prisoners was less harsh than the men had anticipated: 'At first we were well treated, given a good deal of liberty and sometimes taken on route marches.'[37]

Prisoners were brought to London in June and cross-examined by the Enemy Aliens Advisory Committee (the Sankey Committee). Its role was to provide a judicial basis for internment by having a judge individually interview each prisoner in the presence of members of the political establishment. Internees were brought to Wormwood Scrubs in batches, with most interviews lasting only a matter of minutes. The more politicised leaders realised the political nature of the exercise and treated the process as a farce. However, many prisoners sought their freedom and solicited character references from nationalist MPs who were willing to attend on their behalf. Many interviewees gave undertakings not to become involved

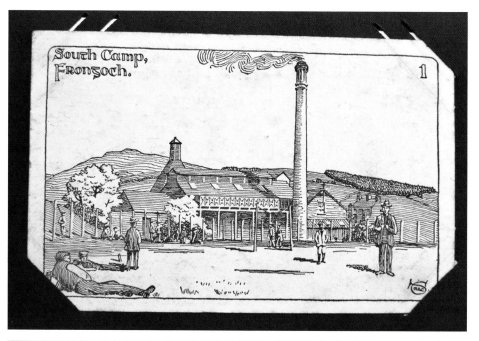

Two sketches of Frongoch internment camp in north Wales, drawn by republican inmates. The camp was a disused distillery and prisoners suffered from damp and cold. NLI

in 'political subversion' in the hope of being released. The commission sought to depict the prisoners as unwilling dupes of the Volunteer leadership, seduced into a violent rebellion of which they had no prior knowledge. The tactic was undermined by the obvious pride displayed by the prisoners in their participation in the Rising, their unwillingness to condemn their leadership and their general hostile demeanour. The commission was regarded by nationalists in Ireland as an attempt to discredit the Rebellion and it backfired for the Irish Parliamentary Party, which had sent its MP John Mooney to participate. The party claimed that it would ensure fair play for the prisoners. Its participation, however, was widely criticised as one more in a long series of tactical blunders by the out-of-touch Irish Parliamentary Party.

The commission recommended that the majority of the prisoners could not be considered a danger to the state and should be released. On 12 July 1916, 460 prisoners 'kept in ignorance by their leaders as to the enterprise in which they had been engaged' were released. By the end of July, a further 1,272 men had been sent back to Ireland, leaving only the most committed rebels still interned.[38] These remaining prisoners were released on 22 December and arrived in Dublin by mail train over the following days. The warmth of their reception reflected the new political climate in Ireland, with cheering throngs greeting many prisoners. Séan O'Duffy recalled:

> On our return, we were received with much jubilation by the people, which was in strong contrast with the hostile send-off. There was a complete change, which was all in our favour. Naturally, we were of the opinion that the cause which we fought for was not yet at an end. Most of those who came back, took up their usual employment but many were victimised and were idle for a long period. The National Aid Association came to the assistance of those who were in distress.[39]

The Irish National Aid Association and Volunteer Dependents' Fund

The Irish National Aid Association and Volunteer Dependents' Fund was formed by the amalgamation of two separate funding bodies to provide financial assistance to prisoners and their families, and to the families of

RETURN OF I.R.A. PRISONERS, MONDAY, 18th JUNE, 1917.
ARRIVAL AT WESTLAND ROW.

Returning republican prisoners being taken through the city on a horse and trap to the cheers of thousands. NLI

dead and wounded Volunteers. The Association raised £137,808 before it was wound up at the end of 1919.[40] The Irish National Aid Association (INAA) was established towards the end of May 1916. Its first committee featured well-known figures from across the nationalist political spectrum, including Dr Michael Davitt, Lorcan Sherlock (a former Dublin Lord Mayor) and Patrick Corrigan (an alderman). Father Richard Bowden, administrator of St Mary's Pro-Cathedral, acted as honorary chairman, providing the association with clerical approval. The scope and professionalism of the organisation reflected growing public sympathy for the prisoners, and local fundraising efforts were the driving force of the association. Details of funds raised nationally were published in the *Irish Independent* and *The Freeman's Journal*. Regional branches tended to focus on the plight of local men imprisoned or killed during Easter Week, and the elevated status of the rebels as heroes and martyrs swelled the coffers of the movement as nationalists vied to be seen to be generous. Significant sums came from the Irish community in America. The Irish Relief Fund Committee in New York raised large sums that continued to flow after fundraising in Ireland dried up.

A second fundraising organisation, the Volunteer Dependents' Fund (VDF), operated separately from the INAA. The VDF was run by prominent republican women (notably Áine Ceannt, Kathleen Clarke and Margaret Pearse) and other widows, sisters and relatives of the deceased leaders. The rank and file consisted of members of Cumann na mBan. The VDF was a smaller organisation, drawing support from the traditional well-known republican families. The VDF was hostile to the INAA and viewed it (incorrectly) as a mere agent of the Irish Parliamentary Party. The prominent widows adopted a proprietorial attitude towards the legacy of the Rising, portraying themselves as the true guardians of the spirit of Easter Week. Their fundraising efforts were far less successful than those of the larger INAA, however. In August both groups agreed to amalgamate, and the Irish National Aid Association and Volunteer Dependents' Fund (INAAVDF) was established. Investments of £1,500 were usually made on behalf of the wives of the executed leaders, providing a regular income for their dependents. The social standing of the executed men influenced the amount paid. While £1,750 was paid to the Pearse family, Con Colbert's invalid sister received £300. The families of Volunteers killed in action received smaller sums: Richard O'Carroll and Philip Clarke left large families but they received sums of £100 and less.

The work of the INAAVDF was facilitated by the growing popular identification with the aims of the rebels within the wider nationalist imagination following the executions. Somewhat unknown and obscure during their lifetimes, and initially lambasted for their role in the destruction of Dublin, the rebels experienced a fundamental transformation in their reputation after 1916 that was as absolute as it was rapid. The process was accelerated by the willingness of the Catholic Church to endorse the spiritual motivation of the rebels, their edifying deaths accompanied by their priests, and their Christ-like sacrifice for the Catholic nation. All of the executed leaders availed of spiritual counsel in their final hours, and died 'good Catholics'.

PREVIOUS PAGES AND ABOVE: Prisoners being welcomed home from Frongoch internment camp at Merrion Row train station in central Dublin. NLI

Equally noteworthy was the participation of an influential minority of Protestants. The outlook of some of the main leaders, notably Roger Casement and James Connolly, was international and secular, and the 1916 Proclamation can be read as a precocious example of modern, secular and civic nationalism. Nevertheless, the recurring theme of the historical redemption of Gaelic Ireland through the willing sacrifice of the young, the pure and the brave permeated the ideology of the republican movement. Far from being sectarian, parochial or archaic, it proved relatively easy to weld elements of Catholic and Gaelic identity to cosmopolitan concepts of a republican civic culture, rooted in the wider European intellectual tradition.

Thousands of enthusiastic well-wishers welcome the prisoners home to the capital. NLI

The claiming of the legacy of the Rebellion by the Catholic establishment was buttressed by the influential *Catholic Bulletin*, which published a laudatory series on the leaders, commencing in July 1916.[41] Depicting the Volunteers as a respectable Catholic army was inaccurate, but the *Catholic Bulletin* articles on the Rising emphasised the spiritual values of the Rebellion.

Countess Markievicz receiving a rapturous reception upon her return to the capital. NLI

5
FIGHTERS AND SOLDIERS: PROFILES

We know their dream; enough
To know they dreamed and are dead;
And what if excess of love
Bewildered them till they died?
I write it out in a verse —
MacDonagh and MacBride
- And Connolly and Pearse
Now and in time to be,
Wherever green is worn,
Are changed, changed utterly:
A terrible beauty is born.

'Easter, 1916' | W. B. Yeats | 25 September 1916

The Executed Leaders

Éamonn Ceannt (1881–1916) was thirty-four and married with one son, Ronan. He was born in Ballymoe, Glenamaddy, County Galway, to James Kent, an RIC Constable originally from Tipperary and a native Irish speaker, and Johanna Galwey, originally from County Cork. In 1883 his family moved to Ardee, County Louth, subsequently relocating to Drogheda. After his father's retirement in 1892, the family settled in Drumcondra, Dublin. In 1898 he became a clerk at the city treasurer's office of Dublin Corporation and adopted the Irish form of his name. An accomplished uilleann piper and a devout Catholic, he played the pipes for a private audience with the Pope in 1908. He married Áine Ní Bhraonáin in 1905 and lived at 2 Dolphin's Terrace, South Circular Road, Dublin.

Éamonn Ceannt (Kilmainham Gaol), 7 May 1916:

I leave for the guidance of other Irish Revolutionaries who may tread the path which I have trod this advice, never to treat with the enemy, never to surrender at his mercy, but to fight to a finish. I see nothing gained but grave disaster caused, by the surrender which has marked the end of the Irish insurrection of 1916 – so far at least as Dublin is concerned. The enemy has not cherished one generous thought for those who, with little hope, with poor equipment, and weak in numbers, withstood his forces for one glorious week. Ireland has shown she is a nation. This generation can claim to have raised sons as brave as any that went before. And in the years to come Ireland will honour those who risked all for her honour at Easter in 1916. I bear no ill will towards those against whom I have fought. I have found the common soldiers and the higher officers humane and companionable, even the English who were actually in the fight against us. Thank God soldiering for Ireland has opened my heart and made me see poor humanity where I expected to see only scorn and reproach. I have met the man who escaped from me by a ruse under the Red Cross. But I do not regret having withheld my fire. He gave me cakes! I wish to record the magnificent gallantry and fearless calm determination of the men who fought with me. All, all, were simply splendid. Even I knew no fear nor panic and shrunk from no risk even as I shrink not now from the death

Éamonn Ceannt with his uilleann pipes. NLI

Áine Ceannt (née Ní Bhraonáin), Éamonn Ceannt's wife, in later life.
KILMAINHAM GAOL ARCHIVE

which faces me at daybreak. I hope to see God's face even for a moment in the morning. His will be done. All here are very kind. My poor wife saw me yesterday and bore up – so my warden told me – even after she left my presence. Poor Áine, poor Ronan. God is their only shield now that I am removed. And God is a better shield than I. I have just seen Áine, Nell, Richard and Mick and bade them a conditional good-bye. Even now they have hope![1]

Thomas 'Tom' Clarke (1858–1916), aged fifty-eight, was married with three children. His father Charles, a member of the Church of Ireland from Carrigallen, County Leitrim, was a bombardier in the Royal Artillery. Thomas was born on the Isle of Wight and subsequently lived in India where his father was posted before settling in Dungannon, County Tyrone, in 1867. He was jailed in England from 1883 until 1898 for his role in the Fenian bombing campaign and he endured intense deprivation, which affected his health for the rest of his life. Upon his release, he moved to New York and in 1901 he married Kathleen Daly (1878–1972) of Limerick, sister of Edward 'Ned' Daly, also executed for his role in the Rising. He returned to Ireland in 1907, opened a news agency on Parnell Street in Dublin, and lived with his family on Richmond Road, Fairview.

Thomas Clarke (Kilmainham Gaol), 'Message to the Irish People', 3 May 1916:

I and my fellow-signatories believe we have struck the first successful blow for Freedom. The next blow, which we have no doubt Ireland will strike, will win through. In this belief we die happy.[2]

Thomas 'Tom' Clarke. NLI

Cornelius 'Con' Colbert. NLI

Cornelius 'Con' Colbert (1888–1916) was twenty-seven and unmarried. He was born near Newcastle West, County Limerick, the son of Michael Colbert, a small farmer originally from Athea, County Limerick, and Honora MacDermott, originally from Cooraclare, County Clare. In his early adolescence, he moved to Dublin to live with his sister, where he continued his schooling with the Christian Brothers, completing his primary education at St Mary's Place and his secondary education at the O'Connell School on North Richmond Street. He worked as a junior clerk at Kennedy's Bakery on Parnell Street.

Con Colbert (Kilmainham Gaol) to Annie and Lily Cooney, 7 May 1916:

> My dear Annie and Lily,
> I am giving this to Mrs Murphy for you. She'll not mind to hear of what is happening and she'll get you all to pray for those of us who must die. Indeed you girls give us courage, and may God grant you Freedom soon in the fullest sense. You won't see me again, and I feel it better for you not to see me, as you'd only be lonely, but now my soul is gone and pray God it will be pardoned all its crimes. Tell Christy and all what happened and ask them to pray for me. Goodbye dear friends and remember me in your prayers.
> Your fond friend, C. Ó COLBÁIRD.[3]

James Connolly (1868–1916) was forty-eight and married with five children. He was born in the Cowgate district of Edinburgh, to Irish emigrants John Connolly and Mary McGinn. His family suffered severe poverty due to his father's irregular employment as a manure carter, and the young James worked as a labourer. He joined the King's Liverpool Regiment in 1877, serving seven years in Ireland before returning to Edinburgh in the late 1880s, where he became active in the growing labour and socialist movements in the city. He married Lillie Reynolds (a domestic

IRISH REBELLION, MAY 1916

JAMES CONNOLLY,
(Commandant-General Dublin Division),
Executed May 9th, 1916.
One of the signatories of the 'Irish Republic Proclamation."

James Connolly. NLI

servant from a Protestant Wicklow family) in 1890 and moved his young family to Dublin in 1898. He spent 1903 to 1910 in New York and New Jersey where he worked as a labour agitator. Returning to Ireland in 1910, he found work in Belfast as the Ulster organiser for the Irish Transport and General Workers' Union (ITGWU). He returned to Dublin during the 1913 Lockout and became leader of the ITGWU following the departure of James Larkin to America in 1914.

James Connolly (Richmond Barracks), 9 May 1916:

I do not wish to make any defence except against charges of wanton cruelty to prisoners. These trifling allegations that have been made in that direction if they record facts that really happened deal only with the most unavoidable incidents of a hurried uprising, and overthrowing of long established authorities, and nowhere show evidence of a set purpose to wantonly injure unarmed prisoners. We went out to break the connection between this country and the British Empire, and to establish an Irish Republic. We believe that the call we then issued to the people of Ireland was a nobler call, in a holier cause, than any call issued to them during this war, having any connections with the war. We succeeded in proving that Irishmen are ready to die endeavouring to win for Ireland those national rights which the British government has been asking them to die to win for Belgium. As long as that remains the case, the cause of Irish freedom is safe. Believing that the British government has no right in Ireland, never had any right in Ireland, and never can have any right in Ireland, the presence, in any one generation of Irishmen, of even a respectable minority, ready to die to affirm that truth, makes that Government forever a usurpation and a crime against human progress. I personally thank God that I have lived to see the day when thousands of Irish men and boys, and hundreds of Irish women and girls, were ready to affirm that truth, and to attest it with their lives if necessary.[4]

Edward 'Ned' Daly (1891–1916) was twenty-five and unmarried. He was born in Limerick city, the youngest of ten children and the only son of Edward Daly, a Fenian leader and wood-measurer, and Catherine O'Mara,

Edward Daly

IRISH REBELLION, MAY 1916.

E. DALY
(Commandant of the North-West Dublin Area).
Executed May 4th, 1916.

LEFT AND ABOVE: Edward 'Ned' Daly. NLI

a dressmaker. He completed his studies at Leamy's Commercial College, Limerick, in 1906 and was apprenticed in a Glasgow bakery in 1907. Due to ill health, he abandoned the trade and moved to Dublin where he worked as a clerk for a builders' supplier and later for a wholesale chemist. He lived with his sister Kathleen and her husband Tom Clarke at their home on Richmond Road, Fairview. A fine singer, he enjoyed socialising with fellow Volunteers and members of Cumann na mBan.

Seán Heuston (1891–1916) was twenty-five and unmarried. He was born in Dublin to John Heuston, a clerk, and Maria McDonald. The family resided in a poor tenement at 24 Lower Gloucester Street near the Dublin red-light district of Monto. He escaped the slums through education by the Christian Brothers and worked as a clerk for the Great Southern and Western Railway company from 1908, transferring from Limerick to Dublin in 1913.

Seán Heuston (Kilmainham Gaol) to his sister, Mary Bernard, 7 May 1916:

My dearest Mary,

Before this note reaches you I shall have fallen as a soldier in the cause of Irish Freedom. I write to bid you a last farewell in this world, and rely on you to pray fervently and to get the prayers of the whole community for the repose of my soul. I go, I trust, to meet poor Brigid above and I am quite prepared for the journey. The priest was with me and I received Holy Communion this morning. It was only this evening that the finding of the Court Martial was conveyed to me. Poor Mother will miss me but I feel that with God's help she will manage to pull along. You know the Irish proverb: 'God's help is nearer than the door.' The agony of the past few days has been intense, but I now feel resigned to God's Holy Will. I might have fallen in action as many have done and been less well prepared for the journey before me. Do not blame me for the part I have taken. As a soldier I merely carried out the orders of my superiors who should have been in a position to know what was best in Ireland's interest. Let there be no talk of foolish enterprise. I have no vain regrets. Think of the thousands of Irishmen who fell flying under another flag at the Dardanelles, attempting to do what England's experts now admit was an absolute impossibility. If you really love me teach the children in your class the history of their own land, and teach them that the cause of Caitlín Ní Uallacháin never dies. Ireland shall be free from the centre to the sea as soon as the people of Ireland believe in the necessity of Ireland's Freedom and are prepared to make the necessary sacrifices to obtain it.

IRISH REBELLION, MAY 1916.

J. J. HEUSTON,
One of the leaders of the Rebellion,
Executed May 8th, 1916.

Seán Heuston. NLI

Ireland cannot be freed by strong resolutions or votes of confidence, however unanimous. It may be that the struggle we have made will lend strength to Ireland's claim for representation at the Great Peace Conference when the map of Europe is being redrawn. Let us pray that Ireland will benefit from it ultimately. Let you do your share by teaching Ireland's history as it should be taught. Mary, pray for me and get everybody to pray for me.

Your loving brother, Jack.[5]

Thomas Kent (**1865–1916**) was fifty and unmarried. He was born at Castlelyons, near Fermoy, County Cork, to a strong farming family. He worked with his brothers on the family farm until he emigrated, aged nineteen, to Boston where he worked with a Catholic publishing and church furnishing firm. He returned to Ireland in 1889 and threw himself into land agitation in his native Fermoy. A teetotaller and cultural nationalist, he enjoyed Irish dancing and traditional music.

Thomas Kent. NLI

John MacBride (**1865–1916**) was fifty and divorced with one son – Seán. He was born in Westport, County Mayo to parents who were both shopkeepers. He moved to Dublin as a young man to work in a wholesale

IRISH REBELLION. MAY, 1916.

MAJOR JOHN McBRIDE

(Born in Westport 7th May, 1868),

Executed in Kilmainham Prison 5th May, 1916.

Printed and Published by the Powell Press, 22 Parliament Street, Dublin. Price 2d.

John MacBride. KILMAINHAM GAOL ARCHIVE

chemist business and emigrated to the Transvaal in South Africa in 1896. He gained popular acclaim in Ireland for his military career during the Boer War when he organised the Irish Transvaal Brigade in 1899 and fought against the British. His reputation was tarnished in Ireland by his divorce from Maud Gonne, whom he had married in 1903. He worked in Dublin as a water bailiff. On his return to Ireland he became a heavy drinker (the jealous W. B. Yeats's 'drunken vainglorious lout' in his poem 'Easter 1916'), was regarded as unreliable within IRB circles, and was marginalised in the years prior to the Rising.

John MacBride (Richmond Barracks), 4 May 1916:

On the morning of Easter Monday I left my home at Glenageary with the intention of going to meet my brother who was coming to Dublin to get married. In waiting round town I went up as far as Stephen's Green and there I saw a band of Irish Volunteers. I knew some of the members personally and the Commander told me that an Irish Republic was virtually proclaimed. As he knew my rather advanced opinions and although I had no previous connection with the Irish Volunteers, I considered it my duty to join them. I knew there was no chance of success, and I never advised nor influenced any other person to join. I did not even know the positions they were about to take up, I marched with them to Jacob's Factory. After being a few hours there I was appointed second in command and I felt it my duty to occupy that position. I could have escaped from Jacob's Factory before the surrender had I so desired but I considered it a dishonourable thing to do. I do not say this with the idea of mitigating any penalty that may be imposed but in order to make clear my position in the matter.[6]

Seán Mac Diarmada (1883–1916) was thirty-three and unmarried. He was born in Kiltyclogher, County Leitrim, the eighth of the ten children of Donald MacDermott, a carpenter, and Mary McMorrow. In 1904, he emigrated to Scotland where he worked as a gardener in Edinburgh, before moving to Belfast, where he worked as a tramcar conductor from 1905 to 1906. In 1911 he contracted polio and was hospitalised; the illness left him

Seán Mac Diarmada. NLI

with a permanent weakness in his left leg. For the rest of his life, he walked with the aid of a stick. He was romantically linked to Josephine Mary 'Min' Ryan, a member of Cumann na mBan from Wexford. In his final years, he was a full-time organiser for the IRB and his closest confidant was Tom Clarke.

Seán Mac Diarmada (Kilmainham Gaol) to John Daly, 11 May 1916 [extracts]:

> I expect in a few hours to join Tom and the others in a better world. I have been sentenced to a soldier's death – to be shot tomorrow morning. I have nothing to say about this only that I look on it as a part of the day's work. We die that the Irish nation may live. Our blood will rebaptise and reinvigorate the old land. Knowing that it is superfluous to say how happy I feel. I know now what I have always felt – that the Irish nation can never die. Let present day place hunters condemn our action as they will, posterity will judge us aright from the effects of our action.[7]

THOMAS MacDONAGH
(Commandant of Bishop Street Area),
Executed May 3rd, 1916.
e signatories of the " Irish Republic P

LEFT AND ABOVE: Thomas MacDonagh. NLI

Thomas MacDonagh (1878–1916) was thirty-eight and married with one child. A teacher, poet and literary scholar, he was born in Cloughjordan, County Tipperary. Both his parents were national school teachers. As a student at Rockwell College, he considered a vocation before a crisis of faith led him to abandon the idea. He subsequently taught English, French and History at St Kieran's College, Kilkenny. His primary interest was the Irish language, nurtured after he attended a meeting of the Gaelic League. He published several volumes of poetry, including *The Ivory Gate* (1902), *April and May* (1903) and *Songs of Myself* (1910). Seeking wider intellectual stimulation, he moved to Dublin and became resident assistant headmaster and instructor of language and literature in Patrick Pearse's St Enda's College in 1908. His first play, the prophetic *When the Dawn Is Come*, was produced by the Abbey Theatre in 1908. His thesis was published as *Thomas Campion and the Art of English Poetry* in 1913 and he was appointed lecturer in English at University College Dublin in 1911. In 1912, he married Muriel Gifford (sister of Grace, who married his close friend and fellow conspirator, Joseph Mary Plunkett). His son Donagh was a well-known poet and barrister.

Michael Mallin. NLI

Michael Mallin (1874–1916) was forty-one and married with four children (his wife was pregnant with their fifth at Easter, 1916). He was born in the Liberties in Dublin to John Mallin, a boatwright and carpenter, and Sarah Dowling, a silk winder. He joined the Royal Scots Fusiliers in 1889 as a drummer boy, and in 1896 his battalion was deployed to India, where he remained for six years. He maintained a lifelong hatred of the Crown forces following his discharge. On his return to Dublin, he worked as a silk weaver and was secretary of the Silk Weavers' Union. He was also a music teacher and conducted the Dublin Fife and Drum Band between 1913 and 1914. He married Agnes Hickey of Chapelizod in 1903 and was a popular figure in the Citizen Army.

Michael Mallin (Kilmainham Gaol) to his parents, 9 May 1916:

My dear Mother and Father,
Forgive your poor son who is soon to meet his death. I am to be shot tomorrow at a quarter to four. Forgive him all his shortcomings towards you – this applies especially in management of my father's business. Dear father, forgive me all, and you, dear mother, the pain I give you now. Pray for me. Give my love to Tom, May, John, Bart, Katie and Jack Andrews. They must all pray for me. I tried, with others, to make Ireland a free nation and failed. Others failed us and paid the price and so must we. Good-bye until I meet you in Heaven. Good-bye again. A kiss for you, dear mother. God bless you all. I have now but a few hours left. That I must spend in prayer to God, that good God who died that we might be saved. Give my love to all. Ask Uncle James to forgive me any pain I may have caused him. Ask Tom Price and all in the trade to forgive me. I forgive all who may have done me harm. God bless them all. Good-bye again, Mother dear, and Father, God bless you.
Your loving son, Michael Mallin.[8]

Michael O'Hanrahan (1877–1916) was thirty-nine and unmarried. He was born in New Ross, County Wexford, where his father was a corkcutter, a trade that he initially followed. He subsequently moved to Dublin and worked as a freelance journalist for nationalist and literary journals. Active in Sinn Féin, he aspired to be a novelist and published literary and historical works, including his historical novel, *A Swordsman of the Brigade* (1914).

Michael O'Hanrahan (Richmond Barracks), 3 May 1916:

> As a soldier of the Republican army acting under the orders of the Provisional Government of that Republic duly constituted, I acted under the orders of my superiors.[9]

RISING
IRISH REBELLION, MAY 1916

MICHAEL O'HANRAHAN
(Author of "The Swordsman of the Brigade," etc.),
Executed in Kilmainham Prison, May 4th, 1916.

Michael O'Hanrahan. NLI

Patrick Pearse (1879–1916) was thirty-six and unmarried. An Irish-language activist, teetotaller and pioneering educationalist, he had three siblings, William (1881–1916), also executed for his role in the Rising, Margaret (1878–1968) and Mary Brigid (1888–1947). His father, James, a Protestant from Birmingham who later converted to Catholicism, established his ecclesiastical sculpture business on Great Brunswick Street (now Pearse Street), Dublin, after emigrating from London in the 1870s. James, a skilled artisan, ran a successful business until his death in 1900.

A portrait of Patrick Pearse. NLI

Patrick ran the family business for some years following William's departure to London and Paris to study art. He predeceased his mother Margaret (1857–1932), with whom he shared a close relationship. His child-centred philosophy was liked by his students but he found it difficult to make close friends and his closest bonds were always with his siblings.

Patrick Pearse (Richmond Barracks), 2 May 1916:

I admit that I was Commandant-General Commanding-in-Chief of the forces of the Irish Republic which have been acting against you for the past week, and that I was President of the Provisional Government. I stand over all my acts and words done or spoken, in these capacities. When I was a child of ten I went down on my bare knees by my bedside one night and promised God that I should devote my life to an effort to free my country. I have kept that promise. For among all earthly things, as a boy and as a man I have worked for Irish freedom. I have helped to organise, to arm, to train, and to discipline my fellow countrymen to the sole end that, when the time came, they might fight for Irish freedom. The time, as it seemed to me, did come and we went into the fight. I am glad we did, we seem to have lost, we have not lost. To refuse to fight would have been to lose, to fight is to win, we have kept faith with the past, and handed a tradition to the future.

I repudiate the assertion of the prosecutor that I sought to aid and abet England's enemy. Germany is no more to me than England is. I asked and accepted German aid in the shape of arms and an expeditionary force; we neither asked for, nor accepted German gold, nor had any traffic with Germany but what I state; my aim was to win Irish freedom, we struck the first blow ourselves but I should have been glad of an ally's aid.

I assume that I am speaking to Englishmen, who value their own freedom and who profess to be fighting for the freedom of Belgium and Serbia. Believe that we too love freedom and desire it. To us it is more desirable than anything in the world. If you strike us down now we shall rise again and renew the fight. You cannot conquer Ireland; you cannot extinguish the Irish passion for freedom; if our deed has not been sufficient to win freedom, then our children will win it by a better deed.[10]

SH REBELLION, MAY, 1910.

WILLIAM PEARSE
(Younger Brother of P. H. Pearse, also Executed)
...ted at Kilmainham Prison, May 4th.

William Pearse. NLI

William Pearse (1881–1916) was thirty-four and unmarried. An artist, he painted, acted and composed verse. Although he inherited his family's ecclesiastical sculpture business on his father's death in 1900, his heart was never in the business and he subsequently left Dublin to study art in London and Paris. Active in the Leinster Stage Society, which he helped found with his sisters, he was a keen actor and taught art and English in St Enda's

College. He was regarded as amiable and mild-mannered by his contemporaries and lived in the shadow of his more forceful brother Patrick.

William Pearse (Richmond Barracks), 3 May 1916:

> I had no authority or say in the arrangements for the starting of the rebellion. I was throughout – only a personal attaché to my brother P. H. Pearse. I had no direct command.[11]

Joseph Plunkett. KILMAINHAM GAOL ARCHIVE

Joseph Mary Plunkett (1887–1916) was thirty-eight and married. A poet, intellectual and journalist, he suffered from chronic ill health and was seriously ill when he participated in the Rising. His family were well-known land-owning gentry and his father George Noble Plunkett was a barrister, historian and intellectual.

His first volume of poetry was published as *The Circle and the Sword* in 1911 while he was convalescing in Algeria. A nervous, delicate and aloof character, he possessed a profound Catholic faith. He purchased the *Irish Review* in 1913 and became the magazine's editor. He formed a close bond with his fellow conspirator Thomas MacDonagh. He married Grace Gifford (1888–1955) in Kilmainham Gaol on the eve of his execution.

Joseph Mary Plunkett (Kilmainham Gaol) to Grace Gifford, 29 April 1916:

> To Miss Grace Gifford, 8 Temple Villas, Palmerston Road,
> 6th Day of the Irish Republic Saturday April 29th 1916,
> Somewhere in Moore Street.
> My Darling Grace,
> This is just a little note to say I love you and to tell you that I did everything I could to arrange for us to meet and get married but that it was impossible. Except for that I have no regrets. We will meet soon.

My other actions have been as right as I could see and make them, and I cannot wish them undone. You at any rate will not misjudge them. Give my love to my people and friends. Darling, darling child, I wish we were together. Love me always as I love you. For the rest all you do will please me. I told a few people that I wish you to have everything that belongs to me. This is my last wish so please do see to it.

Love x x x x Joe.[12]

Key Figures of Easter Week

Constance Georgine Markievicz (1868–1927) commanded the rebels in the St Stephen's Green garrison. She was also involved in the struggle for women's suffrage, and was very active during the Lockout of 1913. A member of a range of charitable and cultural associations in Dublin, she turned her back on a life of privilege to fight for the rights of the downtrodden. NLI

DICK MULCAHY, T.D.

Richard 'Dick' Mulcahy (1886–1971) commanded, alongside Thomas Ashe, the 5th Dublin battalion of the Volunteers at the Battle of Ashbourne in County Meath. It was one of the Volunteers' most significant victories. Following the Rising, Mulcahy went on to become Chief of Staff of the republican forces during the War of Independence and likewise of the National Army during the Civil War. He also had a lengthy political career and became the leader of Fine Gael. NLI

MISS ELIZABETH O'FARRELL

MISS JULIA GRENAN

ABOVE: Elizabeth O'Farrell (1884–1957) and her lifelong friend Julia Grenan (1884–1972) fought alongside each other in the GPO. Both women were fluent in Irish and members of the Irish Women's Workers' Union as well as Cumann na mBan. Alongside Patrick Pearse, O'Farrell presented the final surrender notice to General Lowe that brought an end to the insurgency on Saturday afternoon. KILMAINHAM GAOL ARCHIVE

LEFT: Volunteer Michael Malone lost his life at the Battle of Mount Street in the south inner city. His small band of fighters inflicted the greatest single loss of life on the Crown forces during the week. Malone was a cabinet-maker by trade and was married with a family. His daughter Brigid subsequently married republican fighter Dan Breen. NLI

LIEUT. MICHAEL MALONE
Officer in Charge of Outposts, Mount Street Bridge,
Killed in Action, 1916

Fr. Albert & Fr. Dominic. O.S.F.C.

Members of the Capuchin Order, which played a pivotal role in helping to distribute the eventual surrender notice on behalf of the rebel leadership, and provided spiritual counsel to the condemned men before their execution. NLI

THE O'RAHILLY.

Volunteer Michael Joseph O'Rahilly (1875–1916) lost his life on Moore Street after being fatally wounded while leading a charge on the Crown forces. He had originally opposed the Rising, but came out with the Rebel forces nonetheless. NLI

Richard O'Carroll (1876–1916), trade unionist and bricklayer, was a member of Dublin City Council. He was shot dead in the Camden Street district by Captain J. C. Bowen Colthurst, who also killed three unarmed prisoners in Portobello Barracks on the same day. NLI

Winifred Carney (1887–1943) acted as James Connolly's personal secretary during Easter Week. A trade unionist, feminist and republican in her own right, she was incarcerated in Aylesbury Prison following the Rising. NLI

IRISH REBELLION, MAY 1916.

Capt. THOMAS WAFER

("C." Co., 2nd Batt.)

Killed in the Hibernian Bank,
April 26th, 1916.

Captain Thomas Weafer of the Irish Volunteers was killed on the corner of Lower Abbey Street and Sackville Street while in occupation of the Hibernian Bank. He was a member of E Company, 2nd Battalion of the Dublin Volunteers, and a native of Enniscorthy, County Wexford. He left behind a widow, Margaret, and a young daughter, Mary. NLI

JOHN O'REILLY
(Irish Republican Army).
Killed in Action at City Hall, Dublin,
Easter Monday, 1916.

John (Seán) O'Reilly (1889–1916) of the Irish Citizen Army was second in command to Seán Connolly in the City Hall garrison. Both he and Connolly were shot dead on the roof of the building. NLI

"CORMLEITH"
IN KINCORA.

MAIRE NIC SHIUBLAIGH.

BEN
BAY.

ABOVE: Éamon de Valera (1882–1975) commanded the Volunteers in Boland's Mill garrison. He was the only surviving commandant of the Rebellion, his death sentence having been commuted to life imprisonment. NLI

FACING PAGE: Máire Nic Shiubhlaigh (1883–1958) fought in the Jacob's Factory garrison. A member of Cumann na mBan, she was also a prominent actress and appeared in a series of productions at the Abbey Theatre. NLI

Major-General Sir John Grenfell Maxwell (1859–1929) was tasked with crushing the Rebellion. His actions exacerbated the political situation in Ireland and he was widely criticised in the wake of the Rising. NLI

General Maxwell was nicknamed 'Conky' because of his rather large nose! NLI

A portrait of Roger Casement (1864–1916). NLI

Roger Casement. NLI

The Trial and Execution of Roger Casement

The trial of Roger Casement for treason at the Old Bailey in London lasted for four days and caused an international sensation. Casement's efforts to raise an Irish brigade in Germany left him open to the charge of treason and implicated him, the prosecution argued, in a German conspiracy that constituted 'levying war against the King'. The prosecution called twenty-eight witnesses and Casement was declared guilty by a jury after one hour's deliberation. He was hung in Pentonville Prison shortly after 9 a.m. on 3 August and his body was buried in an unmarked grave. His body was repatriated to Ireland in 1965 and received a state funeral.[13] The trial proceedings were subsequently published in an abridged form in 1917 by the Canada Law Book Company as part of their 'Notable English Trial Series'.

Roger Casement's speech from the dock

My Lords and gentlemen of the jury, I desire to say a few words only with reference to some of the statements made by the prosecution. As to my pension and the honour of knighthood conferred upon me I will say one word only. The pension I had earned by services rendered, and it was assigned by law. The knighthood it was not in my power to refuse.

But gentlemen, there are especially four mis-statements given in the evidence against me which I wish to refute. First, I never at any time advised Irishmen to fight with Turks against Russians, nor to fight with Germans on the Western Front. Secondly, I never asked an Irishman to fight for Germany. I have always claimed that he has no right to fight for any land but Ireland. Thirdly, the horrible insinuation that I got my own people's rations reduced to starvation point because they did not join the Irish Brigade is an abominable falsehood. The rations were necessarily reduced throughout Germany owing to the blockade, and they were reduced for Irish prisoners at exactly the same time and to the same extent as for the German soldiers and the entire population of Germany. The other suggestion that men were sent to punishment camps at my instance for not joining the Irish Brigade is one that I need hardly pause to refute. It is devoid of all foundation. Fourthly, there is a widespread imputation of German gold. I owe it to those in Ireland who are assailed with me on this very ground to nail the lie once and for all. It was published by newspapers in America, and originally, I think, in this country; and I cabled to America and instructed my American lawyer, Mr Councillor Doyle, to proceed against those newspapers for libel. Those who know me know the incredibility of this malicious invention, for they know from all my past record that I have never sold myself to any man or to any Government, and have never allowed any Government to use me. From the first moment I landed on the Continent until I came home again to Ireland, I never asked for nor accepted a single penny of foreign money, neither for myself nor for any Irish cause nor for any purpose whatsoever, but only the money of Irishmen. I refute so obvious a slander, because it was so often made until I came back. Money was offered to me in Germany more than once, and offered liberally and unconditionally, but I rejected every suggestion of the kind, and I left Germany a poorer man than I entered it. Money I could always obtain from my own countrymen, and I am not ashamed here to acknowledge the debt of gratitude I owe to many Irish friends and sympathisers who did freely and gladly help me when I was on the Continent; and I take the opportunity here of stating how deeply I have been touched by the generosity and loyalty of those English friends of mine who have given me proof of their abiding friendship during these last dark weeks of strain and trial.

I trust, gentlemen of the jury, I have made that statement clearly and emphatically enough for all men, even my most bitter enemies, to comprehend that a man who, in the newspapers is said to be just another Irish traitor, may be a gentleman.

There is another matter I wish to touch upon. The Attorney-General of England thought it consistent with tradition of which he is the public representative to make a veiled allusion in his opening address to the Rising in Ireland, of which he has brought forward no evidence in this case from first to last, and to which, therefore, you and I, gentlemen, as laymen, would have supposed that he would have scrupulously refrained from referring to. Since the Rising has been mentioned, however, I must state categorically that the Rebellion was not made in Germany, and that not one penny of German gold went to finance it.

Gentlemen of the jury, I have touched on these personal matters alone because, intended as they were to reflect on my honour, they were calculated to tarnish the cause that I hold dear. That is all, my lords.

ENDNOTES

1. Introduction: Glorious Forever?

1   For contemporary notions of 'honour', see Margaret MacMillan, *The War That Ended Peace: The Road to 1914* (London, 2013).

2   For a discussion on 'manliness' see Jessica Meyer, *Men of War: Masculinity and the First World War in Britain* (Cambridge, 2008).

3   Martin Gilbert, *Somme: The Heroism and Horror of War* (London, 2007), p. xvii.

4   Robert Nye, *Masculinity and Male Codes of Honor in Modern France* (Oxford, 1993); Nicoletta Gullace, *The Blood of Our Sons: Men, Women and the Renegotiation of British Citizenship during the Great War* (London, 2002); Marnie Hay, 'The Foundation and Development of Na Fianna Éireann, 1909–16', *IHS* 36:141, (2008), p. 53.

5   Neal Garnham, 'Accounting for the Early Success of the Gaelic Athletic Association', *IHS* 34:133 (2004), p. 65; William Murphy, 'The GAA and the Irish Revolution' in Mike Cronin, William Murphy and Paul Rouse (eds), *The Gaelic Athletic Association, 1884–2009* (Dublin, 2009), pp. 61–76.

6   Timothy G. McMahon, *Grand Opportunity: The Gaelic Revival and Irish Society, 1893–1910* (Syracuse, 2008), p. 88; *idem*, '"All Creeds and Classes": Just Who Joined the Gaelic League?', *Éire–Ireland*, 37 (2002), pp. 118–68.

7   P. J. Mathews, *Revival: The Abbey Theatre, Sinn Féin, the Gaelic League and the Cooperative Movement* (Cork, 2003), p. 146; Cathal Billings, 'The First Minutes: An Analysis of the Irish Language within the Official Structures of the Gaelic Athletic Association, 1884–1934', *Éire–Ireland*, 48 (2013), pp. 32–53.

8   *An t-Óglach*, 31 December 1918.

9   Report of addresses given by P. H. Pearse, Bulmer Hobson and others in Philadelphia, March 1914 (NLI, MS 17,634). For his writings on the education system, see P. H. Pearse, *The Murder Machine* (Dublin, 1912).

10   In an influential 1967 volume, the American critic William Irwin Thompson claimed that the 'complete failure' of 'Catholic-nationalist literature' to triumph over 'Protestant-Anglo literature' forced the 1916 leaders to turn 'from art to history and attempt to make the state a work of art'. The rebel leaders, frustrated at their collective artistic failures, resorted to a violent uprising as a bloody act of revolutionary theatre. Thompson's arguments dominated later treatments of 1916, but they can no longer be seriously defended. William Irwin Thompson, *The Imagination of an Insurrection: Dublin, Easter 1916* (Oxford, 1967), p. 115.

11   Johann Norstedt, *Thomas MacDonagh: A Critical Biography* (Virginia, 1980);
      Edd Winfield Parks and Aileen Wells Parks, *Thomas MacDonagh: The Man, the
      Patriot, the Writer* (London, 1967). MacDonagh's major works include the
      plays *The Golden Joy* (1906) and *Pagans* (1915), and the poetry collections
      Songs of Myself (1910) and *Lyrical Poems* (1913). He also published literary
      criticism.

12   MacDonagh, *When the Dawn Is Come* (1908), p. 38.

13   Brendan Kennelly, 'The Poetry of Joseph Plunkett', *Dublin Magazine*,
      1 (Spring, 1966), pp. 56–65.

14   Micheál Mac Gearailt to P. H. Pearse, 9 March 1903 (NLI, MS 21, 048/3/9).

15   Canon Patrick Murphy, House of Missions, Enniscorthy, to P. H. Pearse,
      9 December 1901 (NLI, MS 21,046/31).

16   Quoted in Séamas Ó Maitiú, 'A Spent Force? *An Claidheamh Soluis* and the
      Gaelic League in Dublin, 1898–1913' in Francis Devine (ed.), *A Capital in
      Conflict: Dublin City and the 1913 Lockout* (Dublin, 2013), pp. 281–309.

17   Roger Casement, 'Quo Vadis? A Treatise on the Political Situation in
      Ireland' (NLI, MS 13,159/2).

18   Elaine Sisson, *Pearse's Patriots: St Enda's and the Cult of Boyhood* (Cork, 2004).

19   Report of addresses given by P. H. Pearse, Bulmer Hobson and others in
      Philadelphia, March 1914 (NLI, MS 17,634).

20   P. H. Pearse, *From a Hermitage* (Pearse Papers, NLI, MS 21,062).

21   Memorandum prepared by Eoin Mac Néill for a meeting of Irish
      Volunteer staff, March 1916 (Bulmer Hobson Papers, NLI, MS 13,174/15).

22   Roger Casement, Rio de Janeiro, to Bulmer Hobson, 23 December 1909
      (NLI, MS 13,158/6/6).

23   Draft essay by Joseph Mary Plunkett, undated (Plunkett Papers, NLI, MS
      10,999/5/26).

24   Michael Laffan, *The Resurrection of Ireland: The Sinn Féin Party, 1916–1923*
      (Cambridge, 1999), p. 3.

25   Senia Pašeta, 'Nationalist Responses to Two Royal Visits to Ireland 1900
      and 1903', *IHS*, 31:124 (1999), pp. 388–504.

26   *Southern Star*, 7 April 1900; *Irish Daily Independent*, 4 April 1900.

27   *The Freeman's Journal*, 4 April 1900.

28   *Southern Star*, 21 April 1900.

29   Marnie Hay, *Bulmer Hobson and the Nationalist Movement in Twentieth-Century
      Ireland* (Manchester, 2009), p. 46.

30   James Connolly, 'Nationalism and Socialism', *Shan Van Vocht*, January 1897.

31   Patrick Maume, *The Long Gestation: Irish Nationalist Life, 1891–1918* (Dublin, 1999), p. 29; Mathews, *op. cit.*, pp. 66–91.

32   Francis Costello, *The Irish Revolution and its Aftermath, 1916–1923* (Dublin, 2003), pp. 1–29.

33   David Fitzpatrick, *Politics and Irish Life, 1913–1921: Provincial Experience of War and Revolution* (Cork, 1977), p. 72.

34   Donal Lowry, 'Thomas Michael Kettle', *DIB*, pp. 164–7.

35   Matthew Kelly, 'Parnell's Old Brigade: The Redmondite-Fenian Nexus in the 1890s', *IHS*, 33:130 (2002), pp. 209–32; Fergal McCluskey, 'Fenians, Ribbonmen and Popular Ideology: East Tyrone, 1906–1919', *IHS*, 37:130 (2010), p. 63.

36   Maume, *op. cit.*, p. 6.

37   Dermot Meleady, *Redmond, the Parnellite* (Cork, 2008), p. 336.

38   Michael Wheatly, 'John Redmond and Federalism in 1910', *IHS*, 32:127 (2001), p. 343; David Fitzpatrick, *The Two Irelands, 1912–1939* (Oxford, 1998), p. 13.

39   Stephen Gwynn, *John Redmond's Last Years* (London, 1919), pp. 60–1.

40   Senia Pašeta, *Before the Revolution: Nationalism, Social Change and Ireland's Catholic Elite, 1879–1922* (Cork, 1999), p. 153.

41   Ronan Fanning, *Fatal Path: British Government and Irish Revolution, 1910–1922* (London, 2013), pp. 53–75.

42   Declan Kiberd, *Inventing Ireland: The Literature of Modern Ireland* (London, 1995), p. 138.

43   Sean O'Casey, *Autobiography, Volume 3: Drums under the Window* (London, 1945), p. 24.

44   Arthur Mitchell, *Labour in Irish Politics, 1890–1930* (Dublin, 1974), p. 27.

45   Emmet Larkin, 'Taking its Natural Place: Labour and the Third Home Rule Crisis, 1912–1914', *Saothar,* 37 (2012), p. 31.

46   Emmet O'Connor, *A Labour History of Ireland, 1824–2000* (Dublin, 2011), p. 65.

47   *Irish Independent*, 10 July 1911.

48   *The Irish Times*, 8 July 1911.

49   *Sinn Féin*, 8 July 1911.

50   *The Irish Worker*, 15 July 1911.

51   *Ibid.*

52   *The Irish Worker,* 8 July 1911.

53   Pamphlet issued by the Dublin Branch of the Socialist Party on the Dublin visit of George V, July 1911 (NLI, MS 17,102).

54   Richard Davis, *Arthur Griffith and Non-Violent Sinn Féin* (Kerry, 1974), pp. 17–36.

55   *Sinn Féin*, 15 July 1911.

56   *Irish Freedom*, July 1911.

57   Diarmuid Lynch, *The IRB and the 1916 Insurrection* (Cork, 1957), pp. 22, 24; Kevin B. Nowlan, 'Tom Clarke, MacDermott and the IRB' in F. X. Martin (ed.), *Leaders and Men of the Easter Rising: Dublin 1916* (Dublin, 1967), p. 111.

58   For the intrigues within the IRB at this time, see BMH/WS, 111, Denis McCullough and BMH/WS, 300, Bulmer Hobson.

59   Fanning, *op. cit.*, p. 11.

60   Timothy Bowman, *Carson's Army: The Ulster Volunteer Force, 1910–1922* (Manchester, 2007), p. 19.

61   Diarmaid Ferriter, *Lovers of Liberty? Local Government in Twentieth Century Ireland* (Dublin, 2001).

62   On the Irish Parliamentary Party, see Maume, *op. cit.* and Michael Wheatley, *Nationalism and the Irish Party: Provincial Ireland 1910–1916* (Oxford, 2005).

63   For case studies of regional local government, see Matthew Potter, *The Government and the People of Limerick: The History of Limerick Corporation/City Council, 1197–2006* (Limerick, 2006), pp. 351–408; William Creedon (ed.), *Exemplar Hiberniae: 100 Years of Local Government in County Wexford* (Wexford, 1999); Denis Boyle, *A History of Meath Council Council, 1899–1999* (Navan, 1999).

64   Michael Laffan, 'John Redmond', *DIB*.

65   John Redmond quoted in 'What Ireland Wants', *Review of Reviews* (December 1910), p. 569.

66   Lawrence William White, 'Charles Joseph Dolan', *DIB*.

67   Michael Laffan, 'Arthur Griffith', *DIB*; Donal McCartney, 'The Sinn Féin Movement' in Nolan (ed.), *The Making of 1916*, pp. 31–50.

68   Lecture by Éamonn Ceannt on 'Constitutional Agitation', to the Irish Socialist Party of Ireland at the Antient Concert Rooms, Dublin, 10 March 1912 (Ceannt/O'Brennan Papers, NLI, MS 13,069/47).

69   The Sinn Féin Constitution, 1917 (Éamon Martin Papers, NLI, MS 49,485/1).

70   Rev. J. Clancy, *The Failure of Parliamentarianism*, Sinn Féin Pamphlets, Clare Series, No. 2, December 1917, p. 33.

71   Clancy, *op. cit.*

72   *United Irish League: Object, Constitution and Rules* (Éamon Martin Papers, NLI, MS 49,485/1).

73   The Sinn Féin Constitution, 1917 (Éamon Martin Papers, NLI, MS 49,485/1).

74   D. George Boyce, 'A First World War Transition: State and Citizen in Ireland, 1914–19', D. G. Boyce & Alan O'Day (eds), *Ireland in Transition, 1867–1921* (London, 2004), p. 109.

75   Fanning, *op. cit.*

76   Patrick Maume and Thomas Charles-Edwards, 'Eoin Mac Néill', *DIB*.

77   Bulmer Hobson, 'Foundation and Growth of the Irish Volunteers, 1913–1914', F. X. Martin (ed.), *The Irish Volunteers, 1913–1915: Recollections and Documents* (Dublin, 1963), p. 24; Marnie Hay, *Bulmer Hobson and the Nationalist Movement in Twentieth-Century Ireland* (Manchester, 2009).

78   Michael Joseph O'Rahilly, *The Secret History of the Irish Volunteers* (Dublin, 1915), p. 4.

79   Manifesto of the Irish Volunteers, reissued June 1914 (Bulmer Hobson Papers, NLI, MS 13,174/2/1).

80   Manifesto of the Irish Volunteers, 25 November 1913 (The O'Rahilly Papers, UCDA, P102/448).

81   Hobson, *op. cit.*, pp. 28, 30–1.

82   Fearghal McGarry, *Rebels: Voices from the Easter Rising* (Dublin, 2011).

83   Inspector General's monthly report for January 1914, CO 904/91, TNA, Kew.

84   *Ibid.*

85   Synopsis of county inspectors' monthly reports for January 1914, CO 904/91, TNA, Kew.

86   Synopsis of county inspectors' monthly reports for July 1914, CO 904/94, TNA, Kew.

87   Inspector General's monthly report for July 1914, CO 904/94, TNA, Kew.

88   *Ibid.*

89   *The Irish Volunteer*, 3 April 1915.

90   *The Irish Worker*, 25 March 1916.

91   P. S. O'Hegarty, *The Victory of Sinn Féin* (Dublin, 1924), p. 1.

92   *Report on Recruiting in Ireland* ([1916] Cd., 8168), vol. xxxix, pp. 2–4, 525.

93   *Report on the Banking, Railway and Shipping Statistics of Ireland for the Years 1916 and 1917*, H.C., ([1918] Cd.; 9119), xxv, p. 1.

94   Declan Kiberd, '1916: The Idea and the Action' in Kathleen Devine (ed.), *Modern Irish Writers and the Wars* (London, 1999), p. 20.

95   James Stephens, *The Insurrection in Dublin* (London, 1919), p. xiii.

96   Michael Laffan, *The Resurrection of Ireland: The Sinn Féin Party, 1916–1923* (Cambridge, 1999), p. 245; Kevin B. Nowlan, 'Dáil Éireann and the Army: Unity and Division, 1919–1921' in T. D. Williams (ed.), *The Irish Struggle, 1916–1926* (London, 1966), pp. 67–77.

97   Deirdre McMahon, *The Moynihan Brothers in Peace and War, 1908–1918: Their New Ireland* (Dublin, 2004), p. 122.

2. Prelude: The Gathering Storm

1   Florence O'Donoghue, 'Plans for the 1916 Rising', in *Univeristy Review* (Vol. III, No. 1, 1962), p. 10.

2   T. W. Moody (ed.), *The Fenian Movement* (Dublin, 1968).

3   Maureen Murphy and James Quinn, 'James Stephens', *DIB*.

4   Shane Kenna, *War in the Shadows: The Irish-American Fenians who Bombed Victorian Britain* (Dublin, 2013).

5   Owen McGee, 'Fred Allan (1861–1937): Republican, Methodist and Dubliner', *Dublin Historical Record*, 56:2 (2003), pp. 205–16.

6   Bulmer Hobson (BMH/WS, 30), pp. 4, 6.

7   George Lyons (BMH/WS, 104), p. 2.

8   Circular letter from the Provisional Committee of the Irish Volunteers regarding the attempted take-over by John Redmond, 24 September 1914 (Bulmer Hobson Papers, NLI, MS 13,174/10/3).

9   Constitution of the Irish Volunteers ([1914] Piaras Béaslaí Papers, NLI, MS 33,912/1).

10   For the best overview of recruitment in Ireland, see 'Obligation: "Irishmen Remember Belgium"' in Keith Jeffery, *Ireland and the Great War* (Cambridge, 2000), pp. 5–36.

11   Provisional Committee of the Irish Volunteers in response to Redmond's speech at Woodenbridge, County Wicklow, 24 September 1914 (The

O'Rahilly Papers, P102/344, UCDA).

12   Circular letter from the Provisional Committee of the Irish Volunteers to its members, repudiating the actions of John Redmond, 24 September 1914 (Bulmer Hobson Papers, NLI, MS 13,174/10/3). The document was signed by Eoin Mac Néill, The O'Rahilly, Thomas MacDonagh, Joseph Plunkett, Piaras Béaslaí, Michael Judge, Peter Paul Macken, Seán Mac Giobúin, P. H. Pearse, Pádraic Ó Rian, Bulmer Hobson, Éamonn Martin, Con Colbert, Éamonn Ceannt, Seán Mac Diarmada, Séamus Ó Conchubhair, Liam Mellows, Colm Ó Lochlainn, Liam Grogan and Peter White.

13   Proposed constitution of the Irish Volunteers passed at Special Meeting of the Provisional Committee, 10 October 1914 (Bulmer Hobson Papers, NLI, MS 13,174/1/6). The constitution was subsequently printed in *The Irish Volunteer*, 28 November 1914; Proposed constitution for the Irish Volunteers with covering note from Bulmer Hobson, 6 November 1914 (The O'Rahilly Papers, P102/344, UCDA); First Irish Volunteers Convention Agenda, October 1914 (Ernest Blythe Papers, P 24, 1003/b, UCDA); County Organisation of the Irish Volunteers: Official Scheme (Bulmer Hobson Papers, NLI, MS 13,174/1/8).

14   Irish Volunteers memorandum, 2 December 1914 (Papers relating to the Irish Volunteers, 1914–15, NLI, MS 18,289/5). Mac Néill became Chief of Staff; Pearse, Adjutant General; Plunkett, Director General of Military Operations; MacDonagh, Director General of Training; Hobson, Quartermaster General; O'Rahilly, Master General of Ordinance.

15   P. H. Pearse to Joseph McGarrity, 24 September 1914 (Joseph McGarrity Papers, NLI, MS 17,447/8).

16   Inspector General's monthly report for December 1914, CO 904/95.

17   Inspector General's monthly report for September 1914, CO 904/94.

18   Simon Donnelly (BMH/WS, 433), p. 13.

19   Éamon Bulfin (BMH/WS, 497), p. 3.

20   Tom Byrne (BMH/WS, 564), p. 15.

21   Marnie Hay, 'Moulding the Future: Na Fianna Éireann and its Members, 1909–23' in *Studies* (Winter, 2011), pp. 441–54; *Idem.*, 'The Foundation and Development of Na Fianna Éireann' in *IHS*, xxvi (2008), pp. 53–71.

22   Bulmer Hobson (BMH/WS, 31), p. 3.

23   Hay (2011), *op. cit.*, p. 442.

24   Bulmer Hobson (BMH/WS, 31), p. 3.

25   Cal McCarthy, *Cumann na mBan and the Irish Revolution* (Cork, 2007).

26   Cumann na mBan scrapbook, LOLB 161(2), NLI.

27   Helena Molony, Editorial Note, *Bean na hÉireann*, September 1910.

28   Mary Colum is referred to as both Mollie Maguire and Mollie Gunning. Her parents were Maguire but she was reared by her maternal grandparents, the Gunnings.

29   Máire Nic Shiubhlaigh, *The Splendid Years: Recollections of Máire Nic Shiubhlaigh* (Dublin, 1955), p. 159.

30   Cumann na mBan scrapbook, LOLB 161(2), NLI.

31   Cumann na mBan, *The Turn of the Tide* (Dublin, [1915]).

32   R. M. Fox lists 212 members who took part in the Rising and this list was endorsed by the ICA Old Comrades Committee in 1943 (Fox, *The History of the Irish Citizen Army*, pp. 227–32). Fewer members are listed on the 1936 Roll of Honour. Fox's list, however, is supported by the pensions files and is more reliable than the 1936 list.

33   White was the inspiration for the character 'Jim Bricknell' in D. H. Lawrence's 1922 novel, *Aaron's Rod*.

34   *The Irish Times*, 19 November 1913.

35   *The Irish Worker*, 13 December 1913.

36   Sean O'Casey, *Irish Citizen Army*, pp. 8–9. The Volunteers were founded in 1913, not 1914.

37   The text of the constitution was reproduced in O'Casey, *op. cit.*, p. 71.

38   Donal Nevin, 'The Irish Citizen Army' in Edwards and Pyle (eds), *1916: The Easter Rising*, pp. 119–21.

39   Brian Hughes, *Michael Mallin* (Dublin, 2012).

40   'For the Citizen Army', *The Workers' Republic*, 30 October 1915.

41   'What Is Our Programme', *The Workers' Republic*, 22 January 1916.

3. Easter Week: The Fight for Dublin

1   For a discussion on the plans for the Rising see Diarmuid Lynch, *The IRB and the 1916 Insurrection* (Dublin, 1957); Florence O'Donoghue, 'Plans for the 1916 Rising', *Irish University Review*, iii, 1 (Spring, 1963), pp. 3–21; Michael T. Foy and Brian Barton, *The Easter Rising* (Stroud, 1999), pp. 11–72.

2   Simon Donnelly (BMH/WS, 433), unpaginated.

3   Frank Robbins (BMH/WS, 585), p. 66.

4   Helena Molony (BMH/WS, 391), p. 32.

5   O'Donoghue, *op. cit.*, pp. 1, 3, 19.

6   James Slattery (BMH/WS, 445), p. 1.

7   Vincent Byrne (BMH/WS, 423), p. 3.

8   Frank Robbins (BMH/WS, 585) p. 73.

9   Andrew McDonnell (BMH/WS, 1,768), pp. 12–13.

10   Joseph O'Connor (BMH/WS, 157), p. 35.

11   Seán Cody (BMH/WS, 1035), p. 12.

12   Nicholas Laffan (BMH/WS, 201), pp. 8–9.

13   Éamon Bulfin (BMH/WS, 497), p. 7.

14   *Ibid.* p. 9.

15   Frank Burke (BMH/WS, 694), p. 13.

16   Joseph Good (BMH/WS, 388), p. 9.

17   Éamon Bulfin (BMH/WS, 497), p. 18.

18   Joseph Good, (BMH/WS, 388), p. 8.

19   Peadar Bracken (BMH/WS, 361), p. 8.

20   Frank Thornton (BMH/WS, 510), pp. 21–2.

21   Helena Molony (BMH/WS, 391), pp. 34–5.

22   P. Colgan, 'The Maynooth Volunteers in 1916', *An t-Óglach*, 8 May 1926, p. 4.

23   Fox, *op. cit.*, p. 151.

24   Helena Molony (BMH/WS, 391), pp. 37–8.

25   *Ibid.*, p. 39.

26   Foy and Barton, *op. cit.*, pp. 129–47; McGarry, *op. cit.*, pp. 133, 148, 157, 175, 190, 193; Townshend, *op. cit.*, pp. 172–3, 176, 183–4, 189; Ray Bateson, *They Died by Pearse's Side* (Dublin, 2010), pp. 41–65.

27   James Foran (BMH/WS, 243), p. 4.

28   Dan O'Riordan, 29 June 1935 (MA/MSPC/RO/11); Pádraig Ó Ceallaigh, 'Jacob's Factory area', *Capuchin Annual* (1966), pp. 214–19; Sceilg, 'Jacob's Factory' in *Dublin's Fighting Story*, pp. 38–41.

29   Seosamh de Brún (BMH/WS, 312), pp. 6–7.

30   Pádraig O'Kelly (BMH/WS, 376), p. 3.

31   Seosamh de Brún (BMH/WS, 312), pp. 8, 4–5.

32   John MacDonagh (BMH/WS, 532), p. 10.

33   Nora O'Daly, 'Cumann na mBan in Stephen's Green and in the College of Surgeons', *An t-Óglach* (April 1926), pp. 3–6; Liam Ó Briain, 'Saint Stephen's Green Area', *Capuchin Annual* (1966), pp. 219–37; Frank Robbins, *Under the Starry Plough: Recollections of the Irish Citizen Army* (1978), pp. 82–132; 'Labour and Easter Week 1916', *Dublin Historical Record* (1974), pp. 21–9; Fox, *op. cit.*, pp. 156–67; Margaret Skinnider, 'Easter Week, 1916', *Irish Press* (9 April 1966).

34   Frank Robbins, 'Personal Memories of 1916', *Donegal Annual*, vii, 1 (1966), pp. 12–25; Mary Donnelly, 'With the Citizen Army in St Stephen's Green', *An Phoblacht* (19 April 1930).

35   Frank Robbins (BMH/WS, 585), p. 48.

36   Fox, *op. cit.*, p. 158.

37   Frank Robbins (BMH/WS, 585), pp. 70–1, 72.

38   Joseph M. O'Byrne (BMH/WS, 160), p. 1.

39   Andrew McDonnell (BMH/WS, 1768), p. 7.

40   Seán Byrne (BMH/WS, 422), pp. 7, 13.

41   Seán O'Shea (BMH/WS, 129), p. 8.

42   Joseph M. O'Byrne (BMH/WS, 160), p. 10

43   Andrew McDonnell (BMH/WS, 1768), p. 9.

44   John J. Reynolds, 'Four Courts and North King Street Area in 1916', *An t-Óglach*, 15 May 1926, p. 3.

45   Reynolds, *op. cit.*, p. 5.

46   William Oman (BMH/WS, 421), p. 12.

47   Joseph O'Byrne (BMH/WS, 160), p. 11.

4. Aftermath: All Changed?

1   Ronan Fanning, *Fatal Path: British Government and the Irish Revolution, 1910– 1922* (Dublin, 2013), p. 141.

2   David Foxton, *Revolutionary Lawyers: Sinn Féin and Crown Courts in Ireland and Britain, 1916–1923* (Dublin, 2008), p. 69.

3   Maxwell, a veteran campaigner, had fought in Egypt during the 1880s and spent the 1890s in Sudan, departing in 1900 to command the 14th infantry against the Boers in South Africa, where he was repeatedly promoted. He was afterwards stationed in Dublin, London and Malta, finally becoming the commander of the British troops in Egypt. This assignment became complex and important following the outbreak of the First World War as

Egypt became the base for the Gallipoli campaign and the Palestine expedition of 1916. He was recalled home in March 1916 and hurriedly dispatched to Ireland to put down the Rebellion. H. de Watteville, 'Maxwell, Sir John Grenfell (1859–1929)', *ODNB*. A family friend, George Arthur, wrote a biography, *General Sir John Maxwell*, in 1932 and Maxwell's personal papers are held by Princeton University Library.

4   Foxton, *op. cit.*, p. 68.

5   Brian Barton, *The Secret Court Martial Records of the 1916 Rising* (Dublin, 2010), pp. 35–52; Foxton, *op. cit.*, pp. 58–107.

6   A Longford native, Maconchy arrived with the Sherwood Foresters on Wednesday of Easter Week. He led the brigade into its disastrous engagement with the rebels at Mount Street. *Unpublished Memoirs of Brig. E. W. S. K. Maconchy*, British Army Museum, London.

    Major General Charles Blackader of the Leicestershire Regiment, who formed part of the 59th North Midland Division, arrived in Dublin from St Albans to quell the revolt. He was a veteran of India, West Africa, the Boer War and the Western Front. Robin Jenkins, 'Old Black: The Life of Major General C. G. Blackader, 1869–1921' in *Transactions of the Leicestershire Archaeological & Historical Society*, 80 (2006), pp. 11–22. His service file is in WO 374/6285, TNA, Kew.

7   Barton, *op. cit.*, p. 36.

8   The trial of Thomas Kent was held in the Royal Barracks in Cork.

9   The son of a Presbyterian clergyman, Wylie was born in Dublin. A graduate of Trinity College, he was an expert on local government rather than criminal law. Called to the Bar in 1905 and appointed King's Counsel in 1914, he volunteered during Easter Week as a member of the Trinity College Officer Training Corps. Robert Marshall, 'Wylie, William Evelyn', *DIB*.

10   Barton, *op. cit.*, p. 47.

11   Trial transcripts have been published by Brian Barton in *The Secret Court Martial Records of the 1916 Rising* (Dublin, 2010). David Foxton dedicated a chapter of his *Revolutionary Lawyers: Sinn Féin and Crown Courts in Ireland and Britain, 1916–1923* (Dublin, 2008) to the legal framework under which the trials were held. Both books are useful guides to a surprisingly complex topic.

12   While it was traditionally believed that de Valera was spared execution due to his American birth, public indignation at the executions proved the deciding factor. Robert Schmuhl, 'Ambiguous Reprieve: Dev and America', *History Ireland*, May/June (2013), pp. 36–9.

13   'Summary of killed and wounded soldiers and civilians brought into various city hospitals during the Rebellion', WO 35/69/1, TNA, Kew.

14   For insurgent casualties, see Ray Bateson, *They Died by Pearse's Side* (Dublin, 2010).

15   For civilians killed, see 'Courts Of Enquiry into the Alleged Shooting of Civilians by Soldiers'; WO 35/67/3, TNA, Kew; 'Reports of Police and Persons Killed or Wounded by Police, May–July 1916', WO 35/69/1, TNA, Kew.

16   *The Irish Times*, 6 May 1916.

17   *Sinn Fein Rebellion Handbook* (Dublin, 1917), pp. 59–61.

18   Frank O'Connor, *The Big Fellow: Michael Collins and the Irish Revolution* (Dublin, 1937), p. 28.

19   Arthur Agnew (BMH/WS, 152), pp. 4–5.

20   Vincent Byrne (BMH/WS, 423), p. 2.

21   Seosamh de Brún (BMH/WS, 312), p. 4.

22   Michael Walker (BMH/WS, 139), p. 4.

23   Account of the Rebellion in Dublin, Easter 1916, Captain Archibald Annan Dickson (IWM, 01/49/1).

24   W. L. Vale, *History of the South Staffordshire Regiment* (Aldershot, 1969), p. 322.

25   Proceedings of the military court of inquiry held in Room 19, Lower Castle Yard, Dublin Castle, 25 May 1916, investigating the case of the alleged shooting by officers of James Healy and Patrick Bealin, presided over by Colonel G. W. S. K. Maconchy, DSO. 'Courts of Enquiry into the Alleged Shooting of Civilians by Soldiers' WO 35/67/3, TNA, Kew.

26   A. H. Ashcroft, *The History of the Seventh South Staffordshire Regiment* (London, 1919), p. 2.

27   Captain E. Gerrard, ADC 5th Division, British Forces in Ireland 1916–21 (BMH/WS 348), pp. 4–5.

28   Cliff Housley (ed.), *Men of the High Peak: A History of the 1/6th Battalion The Sherwood Foresters, 1914–18* (Nottingham, 1999), p. 7.

29   *A Short History of the Sherwood Foresters, Nottinghamshire and Derbyshire Regiment* (London, 1921), p. 15.

30   *The Sherwood Foresters, Nottinghamshire and Derbyshire Regiment: A Regiment of the Mercian Brigade; Regimental and Recruiting Handbook*, pp. 51–3.

31   James Jones, *History of the South Staffordshire Regiment, 1705–1923* (Wolverhampton, 1923), pp. 417–18.

32   Vale, *op. cit.*, pp. 321–2, 474.

33   Jones, *op. cit.*, p. 418.

34   *Sinn Fein Rebellion Handbook*, pp. 33–8.

35   Seán O'Mahony, *Frongoch: The University of Revolution* (Dublin, 1987).

36   Joseph V. Lawless (BMH/WS, 1,043), pp. 173–4.

37   Joseph Goode (BMH/WS, 388), p. 2.

38   Foxton, *op. cit.*, p. 103.

39   Seán M. O'Duffy (BMH/WS, 618), p. 13.

40   Caoimhe Nic Dhaibhéid, 'The Irish National Aid Association and the Radicalisation of Public Opinion in Ireland, 1916–1918, *The Historical Journal*, 55, 3 (2012), pp. 705–29.

41   'Events of Easter Week: A Series of Short Biographies of those Executed and Killed in Action', *Catholic Bulletin*, vi (July 1916), pp. 393–408.

5. Fighters and Soldiers: Profiles

1   Piaras Mac Lochlainn, *Last Words: Letters and Statements of the Leaders Executed after the Rising at Easter 1916* (Dublin, 1996), pp. 136–7. Typescript copy of the last message of Éamonn Ceannt before his execution is in Lily Williams Papers, NLI, MS 8,286/7/2.

2   Mac Lochlainn, *op. cit.*, p. 45; Gerard MacAtasney, *Tom Clarke: Life, Liberty and Revolution* (Dublin, 2013), p. 287. Neither author provides a source.

3   Mac Lochlainn, *op. cit.*, p. 149. Annie and Lily Cooney were in Cumann na mBan and served in the Marrowbone Lane garrison. 'Christy' refers to Christy Byrne, Lieutenant of F Company, 4th Battalion, Dublin Brigade. Rev. Father Augustine, 'Con Colbert', *Capuchin Annual* (1966), p. 304.

4   James Connolly at his court martial, WO 71/354, TNA, Kew; Barton, *Court Martial Records*, pp. 344–6.

5   Mac Lochlainn, *op. cit.*, pp. 110–11. 'Brigid' refers to Heuston's aunt, Brigid McDonald.

6   John MacBride at his court martial, WO 71/350, TNA, Kew; Barton, *Court Martial Records*, p. 222.

7   Mac Lochlainn, *op. cit.*, pp. 170–1; 'Seán MacDermott's Last Letter', *Capuchin Annual* (1942), pp. 306–7.

8   Mac Lochlainn, *op. cit.*, pp. 123–4. A copy, not in Mallin's handwriting, is in NLI, MS 49,491/2/152.

9   Michael O'Hanrahan at his court martial, WO 71/357, TNA, Kew; Barton, *Court Martial Records*, p. 191.

10   Patrick Pearse at his court martial, WO 71/345, TNA, Kew; Barton, *Court Martial Records*, p. 131.

11   William Pearse at his court martial, WO 71/358, TNA, Kew; Barton, *Court Martial Records*, p. 181.

12   Mac Lochlainn, *op. cit.*, p. 92. The letter was entrusted by Plunkett to Winifred Carney and was later in the possession of Maeve Donnelly.

13   Kevin Grant, 'Bones of Contention: The Repatriation of the Body of Roger Casement', *Jn. British Studies*, 41, 3 (July 2002), pp. 329–53.

INDEX

Note: illustrations are indicated by page numbers in **bold**.